Karen Elizabeth Gordon

THE GARDEN OF ETERNAL SWALLOWS

A Natural Foods Cookbook

Decorated by Barry Zaid

SHAMBHALA • BOULDER 1980

SHAMBHALA PUBLICATIONS, INC.
1920 Thirteenth Street
Boulder, Colorado 80302

Printed in the United States of America

LIBRARY OF CONGRESS CATALOGING IN PUBLICATION DATA

Gordon, Karen Elizabeth.
  The garden of eternal swallows.

  Includes indexes.
  1. Cookery (Natural foods) I. Title.
TX741.G67   641.5'637   80-50745
ISBN 0-87773-186-1
ISBN 0-394-73948-5

Contents

The poet advises: "Read me. Read me again." He does not always come away unscathed from his page, but like the poor, he knows how to make use of an olive's eternity.

RENE CHAR

I wish to thank Micheline Hébert, of
the restaurant Chez Héléne in Venice,
California, for her *recettes québécoises*

others for whatever they did

and the writers and poets who responded in
various wonderful ways to the idea that grew
into this book.

INTRODUCTION

The Garden of Eternal Swallows is about the earth as a basis for flight. And about art as a territory of life: gravity plus imagination, rainbow over barn.

Without sustenance, there can be no thought. Poetry is partly the outcome of oxygen released through the blood and the brain, not only from air we take in, but also from the food we eat.

The same quality of mind which brings two previously unacquainted objects together in a poem also sees or seizes the harmony inherent in flavors, colors, and textures from the garden, finds a way of combining them that never happened before. Every poem and meal is an event in the history of the senses; neither is strictly art or life. Words have a taste in the mouth that speaks them. The act of creating is nourishing and necessary to the process of living, and so is seeing the dimensions in a moment, the universe on a plate.

SOUPS

MISO SOUP

SERVES 8

      1   tablespoon sesame oil
    1-2   pieces wakame seaweed, soaked in 2 cups water 10 min-
          utes, then chopped (use the soak water as part of soup
          stock—it's full of minerals)
      2   inches of daikon radish, chopped in circles, then in halves
          or fourths
      1   large spanish onion, chopped
      1   leek, sliced
     ½   head of cabbage
      4   cups water
    4-6   tablespoons miso

Sauté onion first, then add cabbage, daikon, leek, and continue to
sauté in the sesame oil for 5 to 10 minutes, while heating water and
wakame stock in another pot. Sauté wakame a minute or two with
the rest of the vegetables, and then add boiling water. Cover and
simmer for half an hour. Take out a cup of the broth and cream in
miso thoroughly. Over very low heat (so miso doesn't boil), add
miso broth and simmer for 5 minutes. Have miso soup for
breakfast, for a rush of energy, or as the beginning of a meal.

VARIATIONS: Add turnips and turnip greens, chopped kale and squash,
carrots and daikon, onions and chard, tofu and any vegetables, or scallions raw
sprinkled on top.

ZUPPA GIAPPONESE

a minestrone with tofu and miso

SERVES 6

            3   tablespoons olive oil
            3   cloves garlic, minced
            3   ounces tofu, drained, pressed, and cubed
            2   zucchini, chopped
            2   onions, chopped
            3   carrots, chopped
            2   stalks celery, chopped
          1-2   potatoes, skin intact, chopped
            8   cups water or stock
                half a bunch of parsley, chopped fine
            4   tomatoes, cut up
          ½   teaspoon basil
                chopped cabbage (optional)
            1   cup cooked or canned kidney beans
          ½   cup broken spinach noodles or spaghetti or macaroni
            2   teaspoons red miso
                grated parmesan cheese

Heat oil in a large pot and sauté the garlic and pieces of tofu together. Remove tofu and save for later. Add all the vegetables except the cabbage and tomatoes to the olive oil (adding a little more oil if necessary) and cover and cook over low heat until the vegetables are soft and soaked in garlic. Add water or stock, the tomatoes, cabbage, basil, and half the parsley, and cook gently for 1½ hours. At the end of this time, add the broken pasta, beans, a little more parsley, and cook another 5 minutes. Add the sautéed tofu and the miso creamed in a little of the soup stock, and simmer 3 more minutes. Serve with grated parmesan cheese.

TO A CHAMELEON

Hid by the august foliage and fruit
    of the grape-vine
        your anatomy
            round the pruned and polished stem,
                Chameleon.
                Fire laid upon
            an emerald as long as
        the Dark King's massy
    one,
could not snap the spectrum up for food
    as you have done.

MARIANNE MOORE

CHAMELEON SOUP
SERVES 6

3 tablespoons butter
7 tablespoons unbleached flour
5 cups vegetable broth
2 bunches fresh spinach, chopped
½ cup cream
2 egg yolks, beaten

Melt butter over low heat and stir in flour a tablespoon at a time, being careful not to scorch it. Slowly add the broth, beating it in with a whisk, making a velouté, and cook just 3 or 4 minutes to thicken. When the mixture is creamy, add the spinach, and cook until tender, that is, not very long. Put in blender and blend smooth, return to pan, and stir in the beaten egg yolks and cream. Do not boil, but heat only to that optimum temperature announcing the time to serve.

VARIATION: *Instead of blending, leave the spinach with its chopped integrity—or blend most of the liquid with half the spinach, leaving the other half green and free.*

The same soup may be made using carrots, broccoli, watercress, cauliflower.

THE SQUASHED BLOSSOM

a squash and cauliflower soup

SERVES 2 to 4

1 tablespoon sesame oil
1 yellow onion, chopped
1 butternut squash, cut in bite-size pieces
½ head of cauliflower, broken into flowers
4 cups water
   a scant pinch of thyme
½ teaspoon salt

Heat sesame oil in saucepan and add chopped onion. Sauté 5 minutes, then add squash and the cauliflower clusters. Sauté all of this for 10 minutes over low heat, stirring frequently to prevent any sticking to the bottom of the pan. In the meantime, in another pot you are heating the water to boiling. Add this now to the sesame-coated vegetables, then the salt and the thyme. With low heat underneath, cover the saucepan and simmer the soup for 20 to 25 minutes, until broth is rich and the squash is soft.

Place all the stock and two-thirds of the vegetables in a blender together and blend into a thick golden liquid. Return this to the saucepan with the still-solid vegetables, and simmer and stir another few minutes before serving.

VARIATIONS: Add pressed tofu during final minutes. Serve with garlic croutons and fresh parsley.

CARROTS OF AVIGNON
SERVES 6

```
2   tablespoons butter or safflower oil
1   onion, chopped
3   cloves garlic, minced
½   teaspoon dried thyme or powdered
3-4 cups vegetable stock or water
8   carrots, chopped
2   potatoes, chopped
1   bay leaf
    salt, pepper
    parsley
```

Heat butter or oil in a saucepan. Sauté onion and garlic until they are turning gold, adding thyme and cooking another minute. Add water or stock, the carrots, potatoes, salt, pepper, and bay leaf, and simmer, covered, for half an hour. Remove bay leaf and blend or puree in blender. Serve with finely chopped parsley and garlic croutons and post cards of your travels in Southern France.

A poem should be wordless
As the flight of birds

ARCHIBALD MACLEISH

SANDWICHES
&
SNACKS

SPREADING AROUND THE MISO

Instant Soup,
Instant Energy:

Pour boiling water into a cup where a teaspoon or tablespoon of miso is waiting to take you higher than you are. This is a wonderful lift first thing in the morning, and in sagging or sodden moments of the day.

Sudden Snack:

Mix any of the many misos with cashew, almond or peanut butter, with sesame butter or tahini. Spread on crackers, chapattis, roll into balls with cooked grains. A portable edible camaraderie will sentiently evolve.

A breath disperses the boundaries of the hearth.

ARTHUR RIMBAUD

CAPONATA

an eggplant appetizer
a garden of Sicilian swallows
SERVES 4

1 eggplant, sliced in ½-inch thick circles
4 tablespoons olive oil
1 onion, sliced
2-3 cloves garlic, minced
   several stalks celery, diced
3 tablespoons tomato paste
1 bell pepper, chopped
¼ cup red wine vinegar
1 tablespoon honey
1 teaspoon mixed oregano and basil
   generous handful of finely chopped parsley
   salt
   handful of green olives, sliced

Salt the eggplant circles on both sides. Lay the array of purple-edged circles on paper towels and leave them to perspire, turning over once after 10 minutes and repeating the wait for another 10, meanwhile preparing the rest of the ingredients for this remarkable Italian confusion. Cut the eggplant, patted dry, in small pieces (no bigger than ½-inch square), and sauté in olive oil for 10 minutes, adding onion, garlic, celery and pepper at the end of this lonely time-span. Sauté and stir all of the vegetables for another 5 minutes. Mix together the tomato paste, vinegar, and honey, and stir into the pan, with the oregano and basil and half the parsley. Stir, cover, and simmer for 20 minutes, adding olives any time you happen to lift the lid for a sniff and a circumnavigation with a spoon. When it's cooked, the vegetables should be quite soft. Refrigerate for at least several hours if not overnight. Serve garnished with the rest of the parsley, on crackers, warm toasted pita bread, or on a bed of butter lettuce.

EATEN ALIVE BY TIME
how to enjoy an artichoke

artichokes, 1 per person
whole cloves of garlic
teaspoon of basil
pinch of thyme
teaspoon at least of olive oil
salt, pepper
sprigs of parsley

Wash artichokes. Remove the outer leaves, the loss of a few minutes at most. Bring a big pot of water to boil and add everything named. Cook artichokes until tender, an undetermined length of time, which only you can tell, being there, and interested, and sampling an occasional leaf. Serve hot or cold with anything your heart desires. Find contentment.

THE ETERNAL QUESTION
an egg salad sandwich

hard-boiled eggs, chopped
mayonnaise, yogurt, or tofu sauce
slivered bell pepper
grated carrot
finely chopped parsley
cayenne
vegetable salt or seasoning
sprouts
bread, pita, or chapatti

Mix everything but the bread. Stuff or spread.

CLOCKS

A fama had a wall clock, and each week he wound it VERY VERY CAREFULLY. A cronopio passed and noting this, he began to laugh, and went home and invented an artichoke clock, or rather a wild-artichoke clock, for it can and ought to be called both ways.

This cronopio's wild-artichoke clock is a good artichoke of the larger species, fastened by its stem to a hole in the wall. Its innumerable leaves indicate what hour it is, all the hours in fact, in such a way that the cronopio has only to pluck a leaf to know what time it is. So he continues plucking them from left to right, always the leaf corresponds to that particular hour, and every day the cronopio begins pulling off a new layer of leaves. When he reaches the center, time cannot be measured, and in the infinite violet-rose of the artichoke heart the cronopio finds great contentment. Then he eats it with oil, vinegar, and salt and puts another clock in the hole.

JULIO CORTÁZAR

THE ROADS ROUND PISA
a mushroom flatbread
SERVES 8

Dough:

2 **envelopes dry yeast**
1 **teaspoon salt**
2 **cups warm water**
6 **cups whole wheat pastry flour**
¼ **cup olive oil**
¾ **cup grated sharp cheddar cheese, or part cheddar/ part parmesan**

Dissolve yeast in ½ cup warm water for 10 minutes in a large silent warm bowl; then add salt to 1½ cups warm water, which is then added to yeast. Work in flour with wooden spoon, hands oiled with olive oil, and add olive oil gradually. Flour a board and knead dough, getting the cheese mixed into it, until all is smooth, elasticized, pliant, and uncomplaining. Carry this studded lump to a bowl rubbed with olive oil, shine the top of it with some more, cover with warm towel and let it rise 1½ hours, or until it has swollen to twice what it was, storming the sides of its cradle.

Topping:

basil
oregano
olive oil
tomatoes, sliced
garlic, minced
parsley, chopped finely
mushrooms, sliced
black olives
feta cheese, crumbled

Preheat oven to 500°. Oil a couple of cookie sheets or pizza pans with a very slick surface, take the dough and stretch it and push it over them into a low pale plateau. Sprinkle this with basil and oregano leaves crushed between your palms as you survey the territory below. Dribble next with olive oil, followed by small thin slices of fresh tomatoes mixed with minced garlic. Add another flurry of basil and oregano and parsley, then cover as well as you wish with sautéed mushrooms, some sliced black olives, and more mushrooms. Sprinkle with more olive oil, parsley, and a handful of crumbled feta cheese.

Slide the two pizzas into the oven after admiring the lovely arrangements of colors—the bright, festive red and green of tomato and herbs, the earthy humor of the mushrooms, the shiny blackness like sea creatures of the olives, the whimsical scatter of feta, how the crust already puffs out at the edges like a lost horizon—and bake for 25 to 30 minutes, until crust is brown and crisp on bottom and the top is not too tender or burned. You may want to move the pans back and forth between lower and upper levels to keep the cooking even.

EAST OF THE BEAN

hummus, a garbanzo tahini spread

        2 cups cooked chick peas, or garbanzos
    2-3 cloves garlic, minced
      ½ teaspoon sea salt
        1 tablespoon olive oil
    4-5 tablespoons lemon juice
      ½ cup tahini
            toasted sesame seeds
            finely chopped parsley
            cayenne or paprika

Force the chick peas through a sieve or puree in food mill or blender. Once they have achieved this radiant consistency, mix the chick-pea paste with the subsequent ingredients up to and including the tahini.

Serve in a bowl with toasted sesame seeds, cayenne or paprika, and parsley on top. Eat hummus with triangles of pita bread or raw vegetables, use as a spread on sandwiches with other things, make it a meal, an appetizer, an interlude, a recurrent Middle Eastern guest.

VARIATIONS: Tamari may be added too.
  Serve on leaves of lettuce surrounded by olives and tomatoes.

PIZZA

whole wheat pita bread   olive oil
tomato sauce   olives
herbs, crushed garlic   sliced zucchini
parmesan cheese
mozzarella or cheddar or jack cheese

Warm pita in oven first, or under broiler, on outside part of each half, which are separated. Then heap on tomato sauce, a few drops of olive oil, garlic and herbs, zucchini, and cheeses, and heat in oven until cheese is melted.

CHAPATTIS

1 cup whole wheat flour
½ cup water (or a little less)
**   (salt)**

With flour in a bowl, pour water into a little crater you make in the flour, slowly, and mixing well. Knead dough a while until you feel some life in it, and then cover it and let it sit around and dream for about 30 minutes.

Take a small amount of the dough and with your hands or on a bread board with a rolling pin make it into a flat disk. Heat a large dry cast iron frying pan or griddle, enter the chapatti, turn over several times, and cook for about 5 to 10 minutes, depending on the thickness of the edible little circle. Turn often so it doesn't burn. Make some more.

That's the essential chapatti. It can be elaborated upon with seeds, spices, tamari, other flours instead of or with the whole wheat, cooked grains mixed in with the flour, raisins, a little oil in the dough or in the pan. At some point, it must cease to be a chapatti, if it ever was one, if I'm telling you the truth.

UNDER THE VOLCANO

chapatti
avocado
tomato
grated or sliced raw milk cheddar or jack cheese
romaine lettuce, chopped fine
parsley, chopped fine
yogurt or sour cream (mixed, perhaps, with lemon juice and chili
   powder)
tablespoon of cooked aduki beans
olives (optional)
sliced or grated zucchini (optional)

Slap chapatti* into a hot empty frying pan, and heat on both sides
without scorching its skin, its flour flesh. Turn down heat and
drop cheese onto one side, one half-moon chapatti, flop other side
over, and gently allow cheese to melt. Remove from heat, pry
open, and stuff with other ingredients.

*Chapatti may be the kind you get at the store, of whole wheat, millet, and barley flours;
they are flat and malleable like a tortilla, which you may substitute for chapatti in this
recipe.

swallow   bird of the genus Hirundo
    swealwe   swala   swal(a)wa
      zwaluw   schwalbe   svala
        swalwon   solovej

HOWARD'S MOTHER
SERVES 4

16-ounces sour cream
14-ounce can tomatoes or equivalent fresh tomatoes, in
    either case, cup up frivolously
7-ounce can of green chili peppers
2 cloves garlic, or ½ teaspoon garlic powder
1 teaspoon chili powder
    a bag of tortilla chips or stale or lightly toasted tortillas
1½ cups white cheddar cheese, grated
    several scallions, sliced
    green or black olives, sliced

Another instant outrage. Preheat oven to 350°. Blend in a bowl
the sour cream, tomatoes, chili peppers, garlic, and chili powder.
Oil a casserole, and arrange things: a layer of tortilla chips, the
sour cream accretion, cheese, scallions, olives, and repeat, once or
twice, with cheese completing the ultimate level of desire. Bake for
20 minutes.

swallow   take into the stomach
through the mouth and gullet
swelgan   swalh   giswolgan   swelgen
svelga,   svalg   sulgu   solginn
geswelg   gulf,   abyss   swelgo   glutton
svelgr   whirlpool,   devourer

Oxford Dictionary of English Etymology

DOUBLE CONCERTO
FOR TWO MOZZARELLAS
AND SNOWY EVENING

dark bread
mozzarella cheese
basil
oregano
fresh parsley, chopped

tomato slices
avocado
olives, anchovies
lemon
kelp powder

Take a good piece of dark bread. Lay it on its back and cover its outstretched belly with mozzarella cheese. Get it melted by broiler light. Then lay on tomato slices, basil, oregano, chopped fresh parsley, and another layer of cheese. Melt this one. Over crust of mozzarella most recently mentioned, spread avocado, sprinkle with kelp powder and more parsley as well as a sprinkle of chopped black olives or any other small dark objects (anchovies, mushrooms, capers, commas). Bring down a shower of lemon juice and the opus is complete.

SWAMI ISAAC
a vegetarian Reuben

For each sandwich:

2 slices rye bread with caraway
   many slices of gruyere or swiss cheese
   a handful of sauerkraut
   butter or oil

Assemble cheese and sauerkraut between the bread, heat butter or oil in frying pan, and throw in the sandwich, over rather high heat, until the under side is brown, which means it's time to turn it over, do the same, then cover the pan, reduce the heat, and just let the cheese melt and the ghost of the delicatessen hover as you hold your breath. You have to eat this with dill pickles.

TOSTADA AUBERGINOIS
SERVES 4

1 **eggplant, sliced in half-inch deep circles**
1 **zucchini, grated or sliced**
1 **cucumber, chopped**
2 **whole ripe tomatoes, chopped**
   fresh basil and parsley, finely chopped
   sour cream or yogurt
   feta cheese, or grated white cheddar
   lettuce

Steam slices of eggplant until cooked but still holding together like full moons with purple horizons.

Place the eggplant slices on plates—one or two per person—and top with cheese. Now begin heaping this base with grated zucchini, herbs, cheese, parsley, cucumber, tomatoes, lettuce, and if you wish dribble all this with a little olive oil and lemon juice, or lemon tahini dressing.

Carry to table, top with yogurt or sour cream with dill or chives.

VARIATIONS: *If you are a carnivore, this is delicious with ground lamb, with spices and herbs, or the lovely white breast of one unfortunate bird, as the bottom layer.*

Make a millet base as first layer on eggplant: millet seasoned with pressed garlic and oregano, basil, celery seed, and tarragon, or mint.

Spread eggplant with hummus, then pile on vegetables, and top with hummus, too.

THE MUD PIE MISTAKE
millet burgers with ginger and tofu
SERVES 2

  1 cup cooked millet
  ½ cup steamed butternut squash, mashed
  1 teaspoon safflower oil
  2 tablespoons miso, creamed in 2 tablespoons water
  ⅛ cup cooked hijiki or less
  4 ounces pressed and crumbled tofu
  1 sliced scallion
  1 slice ginger, minced
  1 tablespoon sesame oil

Mix millet in large bowl with safflower oil, creamed miso, hijiki, and squash. Sauté ginger and scallion slices in sesame oil 2 minutes; then add tofu and toss around, almost browning its edges, intoxicating its soul. Add this mixture to millet.

Pour some more sesame oil into frying pan. Shape millet-tofu mixture into patties and fry until brown on both sides and heated through.

VARIATIONS: *Make with cream of millet instead of whole millet. Include chopped onion and any other vegetables, such as grated carrot, daikon radish, parsnip. Try a mixture of grains: barley, buckwheat, millet, brown rice, couscous.*

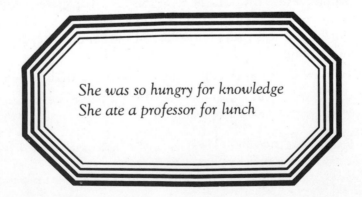

She was so hungry for knowledge
She ate a professor for lunch

THE UNTROUBLED MUFFIN

Toast two halves of an english whole wheat sour dough muffin, spread with raw unsalted butter, and squeeze into the craters and cracks the juice of a lemon. Now fill with one of the combinations below:

chopped olives
chopped tomatoes
parsley
sharp Italian cheese

slices of cucumber
tomatoes
basil, a little olive oil
feta cheese

slivered scallions
sprouts
bell peppers
tahini

romaine lettuce
avocado with chili powder and garlic and lemon juice
thin slices of raw zucchini
grated carrot

tahini (instead of butter)
cream of millet cooked in pear juice and cinnamon (see "The Silken Tent")
more tahini

miso spread
aduki beans
seaweed
sautéed onions

THE DESPERADO

chapatti or tortilla—one per person
vegetables: summer squash, zucchini, little broccoli flowers,
   snow peas, bean sprouts, bell pepper, kale, or other vegetables,
   steamed gently
cheese, grated or sliced
parsley
yogurt
avocado

Heat chapatti in large empty frying pan, turning on both sides, and melting cheese on an upturned flat face. Remove from pan, throw on a plate and stuff with the steamed vegetables, some parsley, yogurt, and avocado, and some hot sauce, too, if you wish.

VARIATIONS: *Omit avocado and add some lemon-tahini dressing.*

Forget the cheese and yogurt and use instead one of many possible tofu sauces.

Spread hot chapatti with tahini and miso mixed together, then steamed vegetables.

Stuff chapatti with rice, tofu, seaweed, tahini, miso, and just a few steamed vegetables such as onion and carrot.

NEW MEXICO SUNRISE

whole wheat bread
canned whole green chilis
sharp white cheddar or monterey jack cheese

Top bread with slices of cheese and whole chilis, from which you have impudently removed the seeds. Top with a sliver or two more of cheese, or a little of it grated, and broil the sandwich until the cheese is melted to your liking. Bread may be lightly toasted first. For special hedonistic effect, top upon serving with sour cream. It softens the chili surprise. So would a bowl of yogurt on the side.

ON THE TABLE

The tablecloth stretches
Into infinity

The ghostly
Shadow of a toothpick follows
The bloody trail of the glasses

The sun clothes the bones
In new golden flesh

Freckled
Satiety scales
The breakneck crumbs

Buds of drowsiness
Have burst through the white bark

VASKO POPA

EGG
DISHES

HUEVOS MONTEREY
SERVES 2

3 eggs
  butter
  diced green chili peppers
  half a large tomato, chopped, or 4 cherry tomatoes, in
    fragments
  avocado
2 ounces monterey jack cheese

Have everything ready: the avocado sliced, the cheese sliced or grated, the eggs beaten and sullenly awaiting the flames. Melt butter in omelet pan, keeping heat low enough not to scald or insult the butter, pour in eggs, and make omelet with slow and deliberate liftings and turnings until the eggs are ready to receive their crown. Arrange tomatoes in red dots amongst flakes of green chili pepper, cheese, and avocado, and if you wish, crush a little dried oregano over it all. Fold in half, and let it rest and melt a few moments before serving. Serve with hot tortillas with butter or sour cream and jicama in lime juice and chili powder.

BABU'S BRUNCH
SERVES 2

4 eggs
  powdered kelp
  butter
½ cup yogurt, blended with ½ to 1 teaspoon curry powder
  half an onion, in thin slices

Have all ingredients ready. Beat eggs with kelp; melt butter in omelet pan over low heat and sauté the slices of onion. Remove onion from pan when translucently golden, melt a little more butter, and pour in eggs. Make like an omelet, which is what it is, being careful not to overcook and dessicate the chicken's gift. Spread half the omelet with yogurt-curry mixture, scatter with onion, fold over, and serve, with chapattis instead of toast.

TOFU TORTA

a cheese pie

SERVES 3 or 4

½ cup cottage cheese
½ cup ricotta cheese
½ cup sour cream
½ teaspoon salt
¼ cup parmesan cheese, grated
¾ cup sharp cheddar, jack, or swiss cheese, or some of each, grated
½ cup milk
¼ cup whole wheat pastry or unbleached flour
5 eggs, well-beaten
8 ounces tofu, drained, pressed, and crumbled or cubed
   oil
1 onion, chopped
1 tomato, sliced
¼ teaspoon cinnamon
1 tablespoon finely chopped parsley

Preheat oven to 425°. Mix the first three ingredients together with the salt and set aside. Toss the parmesan and other grated cheeses with the flour and milk. Add the creamy cheese mixture and the grated cheese mixture to the eggs, alternating.

Sauté the pressed tofu quickly and remove. Add onion and tomato to the oil, sauté until onion is translucent, sprinkling cinnamon and parsley into the pan halfway through. Return tofu to pan for final minute, blending in.

Pour 2/3 of the egg and cheese mixture into a well-buttered baking pan and bake for 10 to 15 minutes. Remove and lower oven temperature to 350°. Spread with tofu tomato mixture. Top this with remaining custard, the cheese convention and eggs, sprinkle the top with a little more parmesan, and bake on the middle rack another 15 minutes.

THE COW AND THE MOON
SERVES 2

3-4 **eggs**
1 **teaspoon honey**
2 **tablespoons cottage cheese or sour cream**
2 **tablespoons sweet butter**
½ **teaspoon cinnamon**
　 more cottage cheese
1 **tablespoon honey**

Beat eggs with teaspoon honey and the first round of cottage cheese or sour cream. Heat butter and pour in the omelet mixture, lifting and cooking the eggs until they are still custardy. Mix the cinnamon, cottage cheese and honey and place on half the omelet, fold over, and serve for breakfast or dessert.

VARIATIONS: *Mix chopped banana, fresh peaches, strawberries, ground nuts, or raisins into the filling.*
　Instead of honey, use Yinnies rice syrup.

CUSTARD DU SOIR
SERVES 2

4 **eggs**
¼ **cup cottage cheese**
1 **zucchini, sliced and cooked**
　 some steamed cauliflower
2 **ounces raw milk cheddar cheese, crumbled**
1 **tablespoon kefir cheese (optional)**

Beat together the eggs, cottage cheese, zucchini, cauliflower, and some of the ragged little pieces of cheese. Heat butter in pan, pour in this mixture, and stir around; keep stirring, and add remaining cheese and dabs of kefir. What you get will be very soft, and stuck together, and strangely wonderful.

EGGS

Kind height, kind in the right stomach with a little sudden mill.

Cunning shawl, cunning shawl to be steady.

In white in white handkerchiefs with little dots in a white belt all shadows are singular they are singular and procured and relieved.

No that is not the cows shame and a precocious sound, it is a bite.

Cut up alone the paved way which is harm. Harm is old boat and a likely dash.

                                    GERTRUDE STEIN

MILLET DU MATIN
SERVES 2

3-4 eggs
     butter
  ½ cup cooked millet
     clove of crushed garlic (optional)
     chili powder
     basil
     oregano
     parsley
     sliced spiced green or black olives and a little of their juice
     raw milk cheddar cheese, crumbled
     mung bean sprouts

Beat eggs in bowl and pour gently into hot butter in a frying pan.
Stir softly with a wooden spatula or spoon. Add millet, herbs,
olives, juice, cheese, and sprouts. Continue to stir until eggs are
cooked but moist and cheese is melted but still in recognizable,
biteable form. As you eat this, the entities become surprises for
your teeth and tongue, and the millet gives a texture sadly missing
from centuries of scrambled eggs.

SAHAD'S BACK ROOM
SERVES 2

4 eggs
   butter
   dash kelp
4 ounces or less teleme cheese
3 chopped pimentos
   parsley, minced
   handful of black olives, coarsely chopped

Have all the ingredients ready to stuff into the pale yellow folds. Beat eggs with kelp in an ample bowl with a wire whisk until frothy. Melt butter in an omelet pan, keeping heat low enough so that butter doesn't sizzle into a tarnished brown mockery of its former self. Pour eggs into the melted butter, and gently lift the edges of the omelet as it becomes one, tilting pan and allowing uncooked eggs to find their way to the heat. As the bottom becomes cooked but not dry, and the top layer still fairly custardy, arrange on one half circle of the omelet the cheese, pimentos, olives, and parsley. Fold over other half, cover pan, turn off heat, and let stand a few moments while the cheese melts.

DANISH ANCESTORS
SERVES 2 to 4

3-4 **green apples**
2 **tablespoons butter**
2 **tablespoons brown sugar**
4 **eggs**
1 **cup milk**
½ **cup unbleached flour**
1 **tablespoon maple syrup or Yinnies rice syrup**

Slice the apples (which you may or may not peel) in thin translucent crescents. Toss them into a pan already swimming with melted butter. Keep the apple slices moving and turning gold. Add a little more butter, stir in the brown sugar, mix for a genesis of a moment, and pour in the egg-milk-flour-syrup mixture. Cover the pan, turn the heat quite low, and let it cook awhile before peeking under and, finding it brown on the bottom, flipping it over. Cook another minute or two on this side and serve with sour cream or alone.

VARIATIONS: *Leave out the brown sugar and let the apples sweeten themselves.*

Add raisins, nuts.

Use bananas, but instead of frying them, drop them onto the egg custard as it's beginning to cook.

Instead of flipping over the whole thing, simply fold it upon itself.

A poem should be palpable and mute
As a globed fruit

ARCHIBALD MACLEISH

LAMELLA PIE

SERVES 2

1 tablespoon olive oil
1 tablespoon chopped onion
  a few mushrooms, slivered
  half a carrot, grated
  stalk of celery, diced
  clove of garlic, minced
2 ounces tofu, pressed and crumbled
1 teaspoon tamari
4 eggs
  a few cherry tomatoes, halved
  green or black olives
1 ounce cheddar or mozzarella cheese, grated

Heat olive oil in skillet or omelet pan and sauté onion for a few minutes, adding thereafter the mushrooms, grated carrot, celery, garlic, tofu, and tamari. Sauté everything for 5 more minutes, remove from pan to a plate, for a wait, and tell the eggs to get ready. Beat them with a whisk and add a little more oil to the pan, which is sizzling with memories of its recent occupants. Pour in eggs, and lift and turn until an omelet begins to form. Lay the sautéed vegetables, the tomato halves, olives, and grated cheese on one half of the omelet, fold and let the cheese melt.

QUICHE DU JARDIN

a carrot quiche

SERVES 3 or 4

Crust:

    ½ **cup unbleached white or whole wheat pastry flour**
    ½ **cup whole wheat flour**
    ½ **cup safflower oil**
    1 **tablespoon soft butter**
     enough water to blend

Preheat oven to 350°. Mix ingredients with your hands and press into a pie plate. Bake the crust for 15 minutes before the custard enters its domain.

Filling:

    2 **cloves garlic**
    1 **tablespoon butter**
    1 **teaspoon sesame oil**
    1 **medium onion, chopped**
  15 **mushrooms, sliced**
    4 **carrots, thinly sliced**
    4 **eggs, beaten**
    8 **ounces sour cream**
    8 **ounces swiss cheese, grated**

Sauté garlic in butter, for flavor, and remove, reject, release. Add sesame oil, onion, mushrooms, and carrots, and sauté until further notice.

Blend eggs, sour cream, swiss cheese, and the sautéed garden contingent, pour into crust, and bake at 350° for 45 minutes to 1 hour, until firm.

Praise with a fork so that the angels
may eat scrambled eggs
on Sunday nights.

ANNE SEXTON

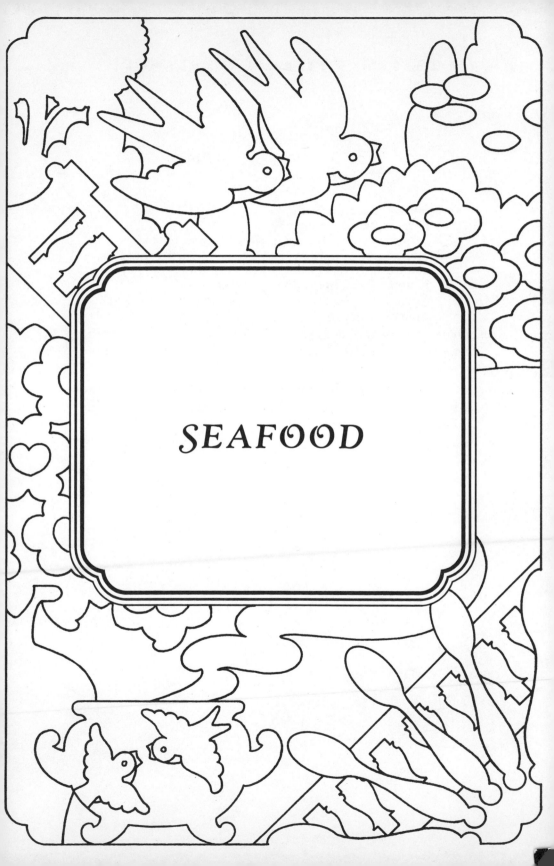

SEAFOOD

CASHEW SEA STEW
SERVES 4

2 **tablespoons sesame oil**
2 **or more teaspoons curry powder**
2 **cups cooked rice (or 1 cup rice, 1 cup millet)**
3 **tablespoons "Supremacy of Cashew" sauce (see recipe)**
1 **cup fresh shelled peas**
1 **pound turbot, in serving-size pieces**

Heat sesame oil in frying pan, and over low flame add the curry powder, stirring and cooking for 1 minute. Now the rice enters the pan, enters the golden dimension. Thin the cashew sauce with a little water, and stir into the rice.

Preheat oven to 350°. In the bottom of a baking dish, with half an inch of water, put the peas and the pieces of fish. Arrange the cashew curry rice on top and all around. Cover with foil or lid and bake for approximately 20 minutes, until fish is flaky and peas are cooked.

VARIATIONS: *For a simpler meal, omit the cashew sauce.*
   Add raisins, onions, lemon juice, yogurt—all, several, or one.
   Serve topped with yogurt and chopped toasted cashews.

SEA CHANGES
SERVES 2

2 tablespoons sesame oil
1 onion, chopped
   scallions, chopped
   leaves of bok choy, chopped
1 stalk celery, chopped
1 clove garlic, minced
   handful of hijiki seaweed, soaked in water 10 to 15 min-
      utes (optional)
½ pound red snapper, cod, or other thick white fish, cut in
      small pieces
1 tablespoon tamari
½ teaspoon kuzu root powder
   juice of ½ lemon
1 teaspoon tamari

Sauté chopped onion in sesame oil for about 10 minutes, adding
scallions during the last minute. Then put in the chopped bok
choy, celery, garlic, and sauté for about 3 minutes. Add drained
hijiki, fish, and sauté another couple of minutes, browning the
fish. Now sprinkle all of it with the tablespoon tamari, cover, and
simmer 2 minutes. Open, and add the kuzu mixed and dissolved in
lemon and tamari. Stir and cook another 2 minutes.

VARIATION: *Substitute a half pound pressed and cubed tofu for the fish.*

DIVERTIMENTO IN SEA
SERVES 2 to 4

         1 pound large shrimp, shelled and deveined
        ½ cup olive oil
       1/3 cup lemon juice
         2 tablespoons chopped onion
         2 tablespoons grated lemon rind
         1 tablespoon red wine vinegar
         4 cloves garlic, minced
            chopped parsley
       1-2 cups cooked rice
         1 green pepper, chopped
            pimentos, chopped

Mix together the olive oil, lemon juice, onion, lemon rind, garlic, vinegar, a little parsley, and marinate the shrimp in this mixture, covered and refrigerated, for half a day. Drain shrimp, keeping the marinade for the next installment, and turn your attention to the rice. Spread rice on the bottom of a shallow baking dish, buttered, and place the shrimp on top of this bed of grain. Decorate the shrimp with bell pepper, pimento pieces, and more parsley, and pour the marinade over everything. Bake in hot oven or broil for less than 10 minutes, just enough to turn the shrimp pink.

THE FISH SCALE

From the Calle de la Acena on, Platero, Moguer is another village. There the seamen's quarter begins. People speak differently, in nautical words and images that are free and pleasant. The men dress better, wear heavy watch chains and smoke good cigars and long pipes. What a difference between a sober, dry and simple man from the Carretería, like for example, Raposo, and a joyful, brown or blonde man, like Picón, whom you know, from the Calle de la Ribera!

Granadilla, the daughter of the sacristan of the church of San Francisco, comes from the Calle del Coral. When on occasions they come to the house, she leaves the kitchen vibrating from her lively and graphic speech. The maids, who come one from Friseta, another from Monturrio, another from Los Hornos, listen to her with open mouths. She talks of Cádiz, Tarifa and the Island; she talks of contraband tobacco, of English cloth, of silk stockings, of silver and gold . . . Then she leaves, tapping the floor firmly with her heels and sashaying her light and willowy figure tightly held at the waist by a delicate and foamy black shawl . . . .

The maids go on for hours commenting on her colorful words. Then I see Montemayor looking at a fish scale held against the sun, her left eye covered with her hand . . . . When I ask her what she is doing, she tells me she is looking at the Virgin of Carmen, that one can see her in the fish scale, under the rainbow, her embroidered cloak open; the Virgin of Carmen, the patroness of the sailors; that it is true, that Granadilla has told her so . . . .

JUAN RAMÓN JIMENEZ

ORIGIN OF THE SPECIES
SERVES 4

Juices of sea and earth creatures combine to create their own broth in this San Francisco Italian fish stew. This is a humble version of a more elaborate and opulent Cioppino, but nothing seems to be missing, really, in the pink shadow presence of shrimp.

     2-3 cloves garlic, minced
          basil
          dill
          thyme
     1/3 cup olive oil
       1 bunch swiss chard, chopped
     4-5 stalks celery, chopped
          handful of parsley, chopped
       2 green onions, chopped
       2 pounds red snapper or other good solid flesh fish, or
          several kinds together, cut in cubes
          whole shrimp—let your wallet decide how many—half
          a dozen is enough and twenty is plenty
          clams, fresh or frozen

Mince garlic and combine with crumbled herbs in a cup. Pour in the olive oil, stir around, and let steep quietly so that the flavors enter the oil.

In a large dutch oven or casserole, spread layers of everything repeatedly heaped on each other, beginning with a bottom layer of vegetables, a dash of pepper, then some shrimp, more vegetables, fish, more vegetables, shrimp, vegetables, fish, and concluding with a layer of multi-colored vegetables, a garden-grown crown. No liquid is needed to bargain with this company. Simply cover, place over gentle flame on top of the stove, and allow the juices to squirt and bubble as the sea changes suffer the heat. After 15 minutes, open the pot and pour over the olive oil and herbs, arrange the clams on top, and cover again. Continue to cook for 15 more minutes, until the clams have opened their shells and your belly has opened its door.

Serve in bowls with a simple green salad and some hot garlic bread or sourdough whole wheat to sop up the herbs at the bottom of the sea.

VARIATION: Chopped potatoes or zucchini can also be included.

*within the clam shell
a leaf of chard
sniffs the sea
a fish bone pierces
tomato flesh gardens
bloom in the belly
of the whale*

TRUITE MICHELINE
stuffed trout poached in cream

trout
green onions
salt, pepper
cream
butter
lemon
parsley

Preheat oven to 350°. Stuff the trout with sliced green onions and salt and pepper. Lay in baking dish and pour in enough cream to cover. Bake, uncovered, for 20 minutes.

When the trout is ready to serve, melt butter, mix in lemon juice, and pour over the fish, garnishing with parsley.

SPAGHETTI GOES TO SEA
SERVES 2

½ pound whole wheat or brown rice spaghetti
½ pound mushrooms, sliced
2 tablespoons safflower oil or butter
3 cloves garlic, minced
1 bunch parsley, minced
1 can clams with juice
¼-½ cup sour cream
2 ounces romano cheese, grated
salt (optional)
pepper (optional)

Boil spaghetti in a big pot with water, salt, a drop of oil. Let it be cooking while you prepare its glorious crown of clams, mushrooms, and cheese.

Saute sliced mushrooms in butter or oil 5 minutes, adding the garlic, *finely* chopped parsley, and the clams with a bit of their juice (not all) at the end of this initial stage. Keeping the flame low, let this new mixture simmer for another 4 or 5 minutes. Now stir in the remaining clam juice, the sour cream, and the cheese, and heat the entire aggregation of agreeable ingredients through. By now the spaghetti is cooked, drained in a colander, and ready to take to the sauce.

VARIATIONS: *Instead of spaghetti, use green (as in spinach, or artichoke) noodles.*

Use half pasta, half string beans, and no sour cream for a less starchy and voluptuous meal.

EMPTY POCKETS
SERVES 2 or 3

2 **tablespoons butter or sesame oil**
   several potatoes, skin intact, diced
   dill weed
   clams—a can of them, drained or fresh if you're on the
      right island
   lemon juice
   parmesan or romano cheese, grated

In a large frying pan melt butter or heat sesame oil, and add potatoes and a sprinkling of dill weed. Keep turning and stirring, browning the potatoes. Add clams, some lemon juice, cover, and cook over low flame until potatoes are crisply softened. Scatter generously with parmesan or romano cheese, cover, and melt, or put under broiler until cheese crust is brown.

VARIATION: Include tomatoes, parsley, shrimp, cayenne, green peas, jerusalem artichokes, onions, and garlic in any combination.

GRAINS

It is not because we cultivate fog! We eat fever with our watery vegetables. And drunkenness! and tobacco! and ignorance! and self-sacrifice!—How far all this is from the conception, from the wisdom of the Orient, the original fatherland! Why a modern world if such poisons are invented!

ARTHUR RIMBAUD

BASICALLY BROWN RICE
SERVES 3 to 4

1 cup short-grain brown rice
2 cups water

Rinse rice in sieve under running water. Bring water to boil in saucepan and slowly pour in the rice so that the water does not stop moving, and the grains keep jumping around. Cover and cook over low heat 1 hour.

Rice seems to come out with a slightly different texture every time it's cooked, no matter how carefully time, heat, and proportions are regulated.

VARIATIONS: For easier eating, increase the amount of water one, two, even three cups. The more water, the more like a porridge it becomes.
  Add salt to boiling water if you need that taste.
  Rice grains can be dry-roasted before cooking, in a large cast-iron frying pan.

RIMBAUD'S APRON
SERVES 3 or 4

3 cups cooked brown or basmatti rice
2 tablespoons olive oil
2 tomatoes, cut in wedges, or 8 cherry tomatoes, halved
   teaspoon of basil
3 cloves garlic, minced
   chopped parsley
   parmesan cheese

Preheat oven to 350°. In a bowl mix rice with olive oil, tomatoes, crumbled basil, garlic, parsley, and put it all in a casserole gliding with olive oil. Sprinkle cheese on top and bake for 20 minutes, until the flavors have permeated each other and your oven smells like Provence.

VARIATION: Make with millet instead of rice.

THE IMMOBILE FEAST
SERVES 2

1 bell pepper, sliced
   broccoli, cut into flowers
1 cup brown rice, cooked
2 eggs
¼ cup yogurt
2 ounces raw milk sharp cheddar cheese or other sharp
   cheese, grated
½ teaspoon chili powder
¼ pound tofu, cut in cubes and drained
½ teaspoon garlic powder, or minced garlic clove

Preheat oven to 350°. Steam vegetables for just a few minutes. In a bowl mix remaining ingredients, except for half the cheese, and stir in steamed vegetables. Pour this mixture into an oiled baking dish, sprinkle with remaining cheddar, and bake for 20 minutes.

VARIATIONS: *Use green beans, eggplant, squash.*
  Add ground sesame seeds.
  Add olives or diced green chili peppers.
  Use snow peas and mung bean sprouts, omit peppers and chili powder, and add tamari.
  Make with cooked millet instead of rice.
  Make with spinach or whole wheat pasta instead of grains.

ON TOP OF MY PILAF

SERVES 3 or 4

      some sliced mushrooms
      a little butter
½ cup fresh peas
 2 cups cooked brown rice
      juice of one lemon
 1 tablespoon toasted ground sesame seeds
 1 tablespoon currants or raisins
¼ cup coarsely chopped almonds (toasted, perhaps)

Sauté mushroom slices in butter and add half a cup of fresh peas once the mushrooms have infused the butter with whatever dark secrets they know. Cook a few minutes and then add brown rice, juice of one lemon, sesame seeds, currants or raisins, and almonds. Toss around in the fragrant butter, and add any herb or chopped parsley that suffices your whim. Onions and/or garlic starting out with the mushrooms gives a headier feeling to this dish.

SUGGESTION: Use this pilaf as a stuffing for eggplant or squash or bell pepper.

LEMON EPIPHANY
rice with spices and lemon
SERVES 2 to 4

- ½ teaspoon mustard seed
- 3 tablespoons safflower oil or ghee
- ¾ cup raw cashews, chopped
- ½ teaspoon ground coriander
- cayenne
- ginger
- 2 cups cooked brown or basmatti rice
- 2 tablespoons lemon juice
- 2 tablespoons chopped parsley

Sauté the mustard seed in oil or ghee for less than a minute, and add cashews, coriander, cayenne and ginger to taste, and sauté further until the nuts are becoming golden. Stir in the rice, lemon juice, parsley, and cook, covered, for 5 more minutes.

VARIATIONS: *Include garlic and/or onions at the beginning.*
  Dissolve a saffron thread or two in the lemon juice before pouring it in.
  Use almonds instead of cashews.
  Add raisins or currants.
  Add shrimp or clams with the rice.

Now stamp the Lord's Prayer on a grain of rice,
A Bible-leaved of all the written woods
Strip to this tree: a rocking alphabet,
Genesis in the root, the scarecrow word,
And one light's language in the book of trees.
Doom on deniers at the wind-turned statement.
Time's tune my ladies with the teats of music,
The scaled sea-sawers, fix in a naked sponge
Who sucks the bell-voiced Adam out of magic,
Time, milk, and magic, from the world beginning.

DYLAN THOMAS

SIMPLY KASHA
SERVES 2

  1 **cup kasha**
  1 **tablespoon sesame oil**
2½ **cups boiling water**
  1 **teaspoon tamari**
  1 **clove garlic, crushed**
     various vegetables, chopped

Sauté kasha in sesame oil for a few minutes. Add boiling water, let boil 3 minutes, reduce heat, cover, and simmer 3 more minutes. Lift lid, add tamari, garlic, and vegetables. Cover, cook another 10 minutes, turn off heat, and allow to stand and steam 5 to 10 minutes longer, depending on the density of the vegetable kingdom members present. Serve with toasted ground sesame seeds, gomasio, a tofu sauce, or nut butter sauce.

VARIATIONS: *Sauté vegetables with the kasha in the first place.*
  Sauté the kasha with an egg in that initial phase.

THE DUCHESS OF KASHA
SERVES 3 or 4

  4 **tablespoons butter**
  2 **onions, sliced**
  ½ **cup mushrooms, sliced**
  1 **clove garlic, minced**
     handful finely chopped parsley
  1 **tablespoon coarsely ground cashews or almonds**
  1 **tablespoon sunflower seeds**
  1 **cup sour cream (or ½ cup sour cream and ½ cup yogurt)**
  3 **cups cooked kasha**

Preheat oven to 325°. Heat butter in skillet and sauté the onions, mushrooms, garlic, and a little of the parsley until onions are soft.

Add nuts and seeds, sauté another 2 minutes, stir in sour cream, and then add this sauce immediately to the cooked kasha, awaiting this moment in a bowl. Put in buttered baking dish, and bake for half an hour. Have some more parsley, on top.

VARIATIONS: *Make with half cooked rye, half kasha.*

Add vegetables, such as finely sliced carrots, squash, red peppers to the onion-mushroom sauté.

Add spices to the sour cream.

SOLITARY MILLET
so when a recipe calls for cooked millet
you can give yourself a knowing look

1 cup millet
3 cups water

Rinse the millet in a sieve under running water. Bring the 3 cups of water to a boil, pour in millet, turn the heat to low or low-medium flame, cover pot, and leave it alone for 35 to 45 minutes, or stirring once or twice just toward the end to discourage the grains from sticking to the bottom of the pan.

VARIATIONS: *For a toasted flavor, dry-roast the grains of millet in a cast-iron frying pan for a few minutes before adding them to boiling water.*

Millet can also be cooked slowly in a heavy casserole in the oven, at 250° for several hours. This way especially it tastes good with a tiny bit of honey—less than a teaspoon—added.

Add ground sesame seeds (toasted or raw), ½ teaspoon of salt, or 1 teaspoon of tamari.

Add chopped vegetables like onions, carrots, and peas during the last five minutes on the stove.

Stir in a tablespoon of miso.

MEDITERRANEAN MILLET

cooked millet
black or green spiced olives and their juice
zucchini, sliced thin
raw milk cheddar cheese, sliced or grated
avocado

Heat millet with a little water in bottom of saucepan, add olives, juice, zucchini, and cook softly just until zucchini is steamed, 4 or 5 minutes. Add cheese, turn off heat, add avocado, and cover for 2 minutes, until cheese is melted. Good for breakfast, lunch, or dinner. You can also take it and scramble with eggs.

VARIATIONS: Alter the title accordingly and make with bulghur wheat or brown rice.

THE MILL

On the other side of because
there ground a Mill.

It was the Mill of Particulars because we heard the word. "When the word comes down, in that respect like the dew, what can we do but wear it?" And so the mill was grinding, and we were wondering away, what grain it knew for its own. "Rice?" we asked it, "wheat or sesame? Simple wheats or millets, kaffir corn? Barley?" we wanted to know. From the mill door came the miller, dusty with his consequences, his face knotted up like the face of a man straining at stool. "Point your words with care," he said. "I have been chosen by this apparatus to conduct the discharge of its energy. I have no responsibility to you or your imagined grains. This is the Mill, and I am the Miller of Particulars. Any other name, borrowed from Fable or Analysis, you choose to give me will be wrong, dead wrong. Why do you detain me from my work?"

We had little hope of learning
more from this man
so we shifted our feet
as we had seen
our grandfathers do
in the old man foot dance called
Becoming the Grass.

"At least appoint a time," our headman cried out, "when we can approach the Mill with what we have, to get what we need." But the Miller declined to answer, and closed himself again inside his Mill. But it wasnt his, we thought and talked, it isnt his, its ours, our own mill on our own ground, worked by our waters. These conclusions were a comfort, so we broke up and went to our own homes, confident that in time the Mill would declare itself clearly, its work and purpose and choice of grain. Meantime we'd grow what we always grew, to eat and make beer from and feed our animals and save some to grow more. And time would tell.

And if time never did,
who among us
would ever notice or recall
when that time began,
to stand out some day
before the mill
to call the Miller out
to answer for his bluff
and grind at last
whatever he thought
to bring with him?

ROBERT KELLY

THE LOST CONTINENT
a mushroom-millet casserole with strands of hijiki
SERVES 2 or 3

a child's handful of hijiki broken into tiny pieces, soaked in water with 1-2 Japanese mushrooms
1 yellow onion, chopped
1 scallion, minced
4 cloves garlic, minced
2 tablespoons sesame oil
6-8 ounces tofu, pressed and crumbled
2 cups millet, cooked
2 tablespoons red or brown rice miso, creamed in 3 tablespoons hot water or part of mushroom-hijiki soak water with dash of tamari
1 yellow crookneck or zucchini squash, grated
2 tablespoons ground roasted sesame seeds

Preheat oven to 350°. Simmer hijiki in small saucepan 30 minutes with mushroom and drain, saving broth to use elsewhere or use instead of water for creaming miso. Meanwhile, sauté onion, scallion, and garlic in the sesame oil for a couple of minutes. Add the little ragged pieces of pressed tofu and sauté another 3 to 5 minutes, tossing frequently to avoid sticking, the natural inclination of tofu, and adding hijiki and mushroom slivers after 2 minutes.

In large bowl, mix the millet, creamed miso, sautéed tofu with hijiki, scallion and mushrooms, the grated squash, and sesame seeds, toasted and ground. Mix with your hands!

Put in oiled casserole or glass baking dish or in individual ramekins and bake for 15 minutes for the little ones, 20 to 25 minutes for the casserole. Serve with a tofu sauce.

VARIATIONS: *Make with brown rice, or half rice, half millet.*
  Substitute cooked couscous for millet, or combine with other grains.

THE LAW OF GRAVITY
SERVES 2

blood of Mexico
sings
pale doors open
fire

         2 **tablespoons olive or safflower oil**
         1 **teaspoon to 1 tablespoon chili powder**
     2-3 **cloves garlic, minced**
         2 **zucchini squash, diced**
         1 **cup sliced green beans**
         1 **cup cooked millet**
            bell pepper or chili pepper (optional)
            tomato
         4 **ounces tofu, drained and crumbled (optional)**
            pinch of oregano leaf
        ½ **cup cottage cheese**
        ½ **cup tomato sauce**
        ½ **cup raw milk cheddar cheese, grated**
            handful of corn or yogurt chips, crumbled (optional)

In large frying pan heat oil and quickly add chili powder and minced garlic, keeping heat low to avoid scorching flavors, then vegetables, tossing and gently cooking for several minutes. Add millet, pepper, tomato, tofu, and mix well, adding more oil if necessary, or more garlic or chili powder if desired, and oregano. Over all, pour the cottage cheese-tomato sauce mixture, stirring, and throw in a little of the grated cheese. Let it continue to cook gently, topping with most of the cheese (what's left). By now the flavors are swimming inside each other, transmuted, rich, past the border guards, carving into your tongue. You can throw the chips in at the last minute or before the cheese spreads its canopy over the colors below. Cover and cook gently until bubbly and the cheese is melted.

BULGHUR BORIS KARLOFF*
SERVES 2 to 4

1 onion, chopped
1 tablespoon safflower, sesame or olive oil
2 cups bulghur wheat
2 cloves garlic, minced
3 cups hot vegetable broth
1 teaspoon kelp or vegetable seasoning
½ teaspoon paprika
½ teaspoon ground oregano
   various vegetables like broccoli, summer squash, celery, green beans, jerusalem artichokes, kale, cut into pieces fit for the mouth

Sauté onion in oil until translucent, and add wheat until both become golden, then the garlic, stirring for another 2 minutes. Add vegetable broth and seasonings, stir, and cover. Let cook over gentle fire about 7 minutes, by which time most of the liquid will be absorbed. On the bulghur nest place the vegetables. Cover again and let the vegetables steam for about 10 minutes. Serve this bulghur banquet with a sauce of yogurt and dill weed and lemon juice. Add some marinated tomatoes with fresh parsley and basil.

*Famous Bulgarian accordionist

THE ORIGIN OF THE PRAISE OF GOD

My friend, this body is made of bone and excited protozoa . . . and it is with my body that I love the fields. How do I know what I feel but what the body tells me? Erasmus thinking in the snow, translators of Virgil who burn up the whole room, the man in furs reading the Arabic astrologer falls off his three-legged stool in astonishment—this is the body, so beautifully carved inside, with the curves of the inner ear, and the husk, so rough, knuckle-brown.

As we walk we enter the magnetic fields of other bodies, and every smell we take in the communities of protozoa see, and a being inside leaps up toward it, as a horse rears at the starting gate. When we come near each other, we are drawn down into the sweetest pools of slowly circling energies, slowly circling smells. And the protozoa know there are odors the shape of oranges, or tornadoes, of octopuses . . .

The sunlight lays itself down before the protozoa,
the night opens itself out behind it,
and inside its own energy it lives!

So the space between two people diminishes, it grows less and less, no one to weep, they merge at last. The sound that pours from the fingertips awakens clouds of cells far inside the body, and beings unknown to us start out in a pilgrimage to their Saviour, to their holy place. Their holy place is a small black stone, that they remember from Protozoic times, when it was rolled away from a door . . . and it was after that they found their friends, who helped them to digest the hard grains of this world . . . The cloud of cells awakens, intensifies, swarms . . . the cells dance inside beams of sunlight so thin we cannot see them . . . To them each ray is a vast palace, with thousands of rooms. From the dance of the cells praise sentences rise to the throat of the man praying and singing alone in his room. He lets his arms climb above his head, and says, "Now do you still say you cannot choose the Road?"

ROBERT BLY
for Lewis Thomas,
and his The Lives of a Cell

BEANS
&
PASTA

For a man like him, holed up in written reality, those stormy sessions that began in the bookstore and ended at dawn in the brothels were a revelation. It had never occurred to him until then to think that literature was the best plaything that had ever been invented to make fun of people, as Alvaro demonstrated during one night of revels. Some time would have to pass before Aureliano realized that such arbitrary attitudes had their origins in the example of the wise Catalonian, for whom wisdom was worth nothing if it could not be used to invent a new way of preparing chick peas.

GABRIEL GARCÍA MÁRQUEZ

THE WISE OLD CATALONIAN
SERVES 3 or 4

1 cup dry garbanzos or 1 cup canned chick peas
3 tomatoes, finely chopped, or 2 teaspoons tomato paste
1 tablespoon safflower or olive oil
1 teaspoon honey
2 teaspoons tamari
1 tablespoon cider vinegar
1 teaspoon caraway seeds
1 teaspoon cumin
¼ head purple cabbage, in chunks

Cook the garbanzos in 4 cups of water for 3 hours. Once they're cooked, or you've opened the can, you may proceed. Sauté the tomatoes in oil until a thick sauce is formed. Or stir tomato paste into the water you'd otherwise add at this stage. To sautéed tomatoes, add ½ cup of water (which could be the garbanzo cooking water), the honey, tamari, vinegar, caraway, and cumin, and stir. Add the chopped cabbage and garbanzos, cover, and simmer until cabbage is cooked. Serve with rice, kasha, bulghur wheat, or couscous.

THE CROWDED CRUST
or the crusty crowd
SERVES 4

Sauce:

    2 onions, chopped
    2 tablespoons olive oil
    3 cloves garlic, minced
    2 teaspoons chili powder
  ½ teaspoon cumin
    1 large can tomatoes, drained and chopped (save some
        juice), or fresh tomatoes, chopped
    1 teaspoon red miso, creamed in 3 tablespoons warm water

Sauté onions in olive oil, adding garlic and chili powder and cumin and mixing them in for a few minutes over low flame. Now add the tomatoes and their juice. Cook, stirring, 5 or 10 minutes, adding miso the last couple of minutes.

Crust and filling:

1 cup cornmeal
1 teaspoon herbs and spices (cayenne, sage, oregano, kelp)
5 cups water
1 cup white cheddar or jack cheese, grated
1 cup kidney beans, cooked

Preheat oven to 425°. Mix cornmeal and spices in saucepan and gradually stir in the cold water, keeping the mixture smooth. Place on medium flame, stirring constantly, and bring to a boil. Continue to cook and stir until the mush becomes quite thick, about 20 minutes. Let it sit awhile, cooling and solidifying for at least an hour. Pour into a greased baking pan or dish and bake for about 20 minutes. Remove from oven, sprinkle with some of the cheese, then spoon on the beans, top with the sauce and more cheese. Bake the whole pie in the oven another 15 minutes, until cheese is melted.

ROCKY HOSANNA
SERVES 2 or 3

½ cup lentils
½ cup lima beans
olive oil
1 onion, chopped

some celery, chopped
1 clove garlic, minced
parsley

Cook lentils and lima beans together in 3 cups of water for 1½ hours. Remove with slotted spoon or drain, saving juice for stock. Heat oil in frying pan and sauté onion for 5 minutes, add celery and garlic and sauté another 5 minutes. Add cooked lentils and limas and parsley, mix together, cooking over low flame for 5 to 10 more minutes.

VARIATIONS: Include pimentos at the end.

Add other vegetables such as carrots, cauliflower, or peas, with the celery and garlic.

ADOBE EQUINOX

3 ways of looking at a pile of beans

SERVES 4 to 6

    4 cups kidney beans, cooked
    ½ cup bean stock
    2 tablespoons tomato paste
    2 teaspoons red miso
    3 tablespoons olive oil
    2 yellow onions, chopped
    5 cloves garlic (or less), minced
  2-3 teaspoons chili powder
    4 summer squash, sliced thin, and then again in half
    1 cup winter squash, cut in delicate wedges
    8 ounces tofu, pressed and crumbled

Take the beans at any temperature and some of the stock together in a blender and alter their shape into a homogeneous mass. Mix tomato paste with the rest of the stock, add miso as well, and blend thoroughly in a cup or small bowl. Heat oil in frying pan and sauté onions, adding garlic and chili powder as the onions approach transparency and exude their natural sweetness. Now add the two seasons of squash and keep things moving in the chili-flavored bottom of the pan, absorbing centuries of southern hemisphere history as the cellulose walls collapse. Next stir in the beans and tomato-miso mixture, and cook over very low heat for another 5 minutes, stirring, then adding the crumbled tofu to the scented simmering soup. Continue to gently cook another 3 minutes, just long enough to warm up the tofu and convert it to the Mayan religion, adding more water or bean stock if things are getting sticky where meal and metal meet.

Uses for "Adobe Equinox" follow.

THE BANDITO'S BIRTHDAY CAKE

Preheat oven to 350°. Warm 6 fresh corn tortillas in oven for 5 minutes. Remove, and spread one with the bean chili mixture, grate with a little mild white cheese, top with second tortilla, then repeat with beans and cheese, continuing until you've built a six-layer cake, sitting in a pan. Pour over the entire structure canned enchilada sauce or "Fernando's Reply" (see recipe), grate on more cheese, and bake for 15 to 20 minutes, until cheese is bubbly and melted. Cut like a cake, in halves or quarters, or share it with your shadow, who will always ask for more.

STUFFED ENVELOPES

Fry tortillas in oil and drain on paper towels, or heat in oven; then spread with "Adobe Equinox." Fold in half or roll like a lost cigar and hand it to yourself in the midst of a bowl of steamed vegetables, a salad, or a good book.

TOTAL TOSTADAS

Spread tortillas, fried, thickly with grated cheese, "Adobe Equinox," more cheese, shredded lettuce, tomatoes, more cheese, and top with guacamole or something else to take you by surprise.

PASTA OLIVERA
SERVES 2

½ pound whole wheat noodles or macaroni
2 eggs
¼ cup olive oil
2 cups cheddar cheese, grated
1 clove garlic, minced
  chopped parsley
1 cup chopped black olives

Preheat oven to 400°. Cook pasta like you're supposed to and drain—more on the *al dente* side than not.

Beat eggs and stir in the olive oil, cheese, garlic, and parsley. In a baking dish, spread out the cooked pasta, and cover with the olive topping. Bake 15 minutes.

VARIATIONS: *Make with cooked grain instead of pasta.*
  Include pressed slices of tofu with pasta layer.
  Add slightly steamed fish to pasta layer, or a can of shrimp or clams.

NOODLES DU MONDE

  whole wheat ramen or soba noodles
3 tablespoons peanut or safflower oil
1-2 teaspoons curry powder
1 cup fresh parsley, minced
1 tablespoon or more ground almonds
1 tablespoon lemon juice

Preheat oven to 350°. Cook noodles quickly in boiling water and drain. Don't overcook. Heat oil and fry curry powder. Remove from heat and add in mixing bowl to the cooked noodles along with the parsley, almonds, and lemon juice. Toss lightly, put in greased pan, and bake for 10 minutes.

VARIATIONS: *Instead of noodles, use basmatti or brown rice.*
  Skip the oven sojourn.

Sober almond trees, olives pugnacious and
dreamy, on the fan of twilight,
post our strange health.

RENE CHAR

VIVALDI'S AFTERMATH
the pasta's garden party
SERVES 2

**1 cup vegetable macaroni or other whole wheat vegetable
  pasta**
2 tablespoons olive oil
1 teaspoon basil
3 cloves garlic, minced
  handful of string beans, sliced diagonally
1 zucchini, sliced thin
½ cup raw milk cheddar cheese, grated
2 tablespoons parmesan cheese
  finely chopped parsley

Bring a quart or two of water to boil in a saucepan, add a couple of
drops of oil, and pasta, and cook over rabid flame until half
tender. In the meantime, mix olive oil, basil crumbled and crushed
into it, and garlic in a cup together and leave them to smell each
other. Add beans to water and pasta, bring heat down a little, cook
a few more minutes, and bring on the zucchini. Continue to cook
another 3 minutes. Drain all immediately in a colander and spoon
pasta and vegetables onto plates, drizzle with olive oil *pesto* and
sprinkle with cheeses and parsley, tossing lightly. Good with
"Satyr's Salad" (see recipe).

VARIATION: Leave out the pasta entirely.
  *Just cook the vegetables until tender and follow the serving instructions with
the addition of cooked rice instead.*

THE ART OF SPAGHETTI

pasta entwined in solar colors

SERVES 2 or 3

olive oil
crumbled basil
½ pound brown rice spaghetti or whole wheat spaghetti
1 ounce hijiki seaweed, soaked in water 15 minutes
3 carrots, sliced in slender lengthwise strips
yellow squash, as much as you want, sliced in long thin
strips
cauliflower flowers
8 whole scallions, ends trimmed
handful of parsley, finely chopped
3-5 cloves of garlic, minced
toasted sesame seeds

Bring a large saucepan of water to a boil, and add a few drops of oil and some basil rubbed against itself, its own fragrances, with the friction of your thumb and forefinger.

Now place the spaghetti into the bubbles, watching it sink and soften. Keep the water rolling and add the hijiki and cook all this for about 7 minutes. Add carrots, squash, cauliflower, scallions, and cook everything for approximately 5 more minutes. Drain in colander, and then mix in a bowl with olive oil, parsley, and the garlic pressed into insistent little shrieks. Upon serving, grind roasted sesame seeds over this bowl of color.

VARIATIONS: *Include slices of bell pepper with addition of vegetables.*
Tofu cubes, pressed, may be added the last 5 minutes, a voice from the protein contingent.
The scallion slices may be reserved for a raw addition at the end.
Conversely, the garlic may be cooked with everything else. It's more than a matter of taste.

CHAIN REACTION
SERVES 2 to 4

          sesame or olive oil
          basil
          green beans, cut in 1" lengths
          zucchini, cut in matchsticks
          parmesan cheese
          parsley
$\frac{1}{4}$-$\frac{1}{2}$ pound spaghetti, spinach noodles, or soba
          a handful of hijiki, soaked in water 15 minutes
          a handful of wakame, soaked with hijiki
  2-4 ounces tofu, pressed and cubed
          sicilian olives
          tahini
          tamari

In boiling water with oil and basil, cook the green beans briefly. Add matchstick zucchini, and cook the two vegetables together until barely tender: let them retain a little integrity, resilience, spine. Remove with slotted spoon to a bowl, and toss with a sprinkling of parmesan and parsley.

To the water, add the pasta. Halfway through, add seaweed, and when it's almost entirely cooked, add tofu cubes. Since soba cooks faster than other pasta, if you use that, include hijiki and wakame from the beginning of its boiling time. Drain pasta and seaweeds, dump on top of the vegetables, mix in the sliced olives, a little more cheese, some tahini, and then make a paste with some oil, tahini, and tamari, and toss the pasta-vegetable affability gently and very well.

Very cross-culturally ridiculous and delicious.

"Calac and Polanco were arguing as usual," I tell Nicole, "but this time the great novelty was that they were doing it in English and about swallows, right in the Underground, in order to get in some practice, I suppose."

"Could anything be understood?" Nicole asks.

"Well, they can speak it well enough now so that several passengers listened to them in stupefaction. There was a woman dressed in pink, naturally, who looked all around as if to catch sight of a flock of swallows in the middle of the Leicester Square station, which must be three hundred feet beneath the surface."

"But what is there to argue about with swallows?" Nicole asks, cleaning a small brush.

"Their habits, whether they put their heads under their wings, whether they're stupid, whether they're mammals, things like that."

"They're so funny when they argue," Nicole says. "In Spanish, especially, you can see that they're doing it to have fun. Do they talk about swallows, too? We'll have to ask my paredros. Maybe there are a lot of swallows in Argentina and it's a great subject for an argument."

"My paredros or Juan," I tell her. "That southern land is so well-represented among us."

Nicole makes no comment. She lowers her eyes and goes back to cleaning the brush; it gets worse every time, every time we get closer to that point where we have to dance prudently around a name, being careful not to say it, going along with allusions or groupings, never head on. And when she said: "My paredros," who could she have been talking about? Why did I have to bring up that other name? But if we don't say it anymore, what will happen to that well, to that black funnel? So far courtesy and affection have saved us. Nothing but swallows now, from now on?

JULIO CORTÁZAR

RED RENAISSANCE
SERVES 2 to 4

1   tablespoon olive oil
2   cloves garlic, minced
1   onion, chopped
1   cup tomato sauce
1   teaspoon basil
    handful of parsley, chopped
⅛   teaspoon ground oregano
    vegetable salt or powder
½   pound whole wheat lasagne noodles or other pasta,
    cooked and drained
2   zucchini, sliced thin
½   cup ricotta cheese
½   cup monterey jack cheese, grated
2   tablespoons parmesan or romano cheese

Preheat oven to 400°. Oil a baking dish. In a large frying pan, heat oil and saute minced garlic and chopped onion. Add tomato sauce, herbs and vegetable salt. Cook slowly until sauce thickens. Spread a layer of cooked pasta on bottom of baking dish, top with slices of zucchini, dot with ricotta, pour half the sauce over, sprinkle with half the grated jack cheese. Repeat, concluding with cheese on top, and parmesan or romano topping that. Bake in oven uncovered for 15 minutes.

VARIATIONS: *Make with brown rice or millet, precooked.*
  Include slices of pressed tofu somewhere in the midst of these layers.
  Use steamed slices of eggplant in addition to or instead of the pasta.

SEED JOURNEY

There they go
and where they stop
trees will grow

The nuts of amnesiac squirrels
more nuts will be
Bur takes freight on animal fur
And pollen the wind does carry

For some seeds
meal is the end of the journey

GREGORY CORSO

VEGETABLES

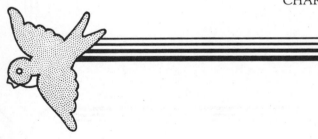

It is my impression that all parts of speech suddenly, in composition by field, are fresh for both sound and percussive use, spring up like unknown, unnamed vegetables in the patch, when you work it, come spring.

CHARLES OLSON

THE DROWSY GREENNESS OF WILD ASIAN PONIES

SERVES 2

    about 6 mushrooms, sliced
1 tablespoon sesame oil
    green beans, many, sliced diagonally or lengthwise
3 tablespoons water
1 teaspoon tamari
    garlic powder or minced fresh garlic
    fresh peas
8 ounces tofu, cubed

Sauté mushrooms in oil over low fire. Add green beans, water, the tamari and garlic, and simmer, covered, 4 minutes. Add peas and tofu, recover, and simmer another 3 minutes.

This makes a light meal with a dark flavor.

TOMATOES PROVENÇAL

parsley, chopped fine
bread crumbs
minced garlic
salt
pepper
olive oil and butter, equal amounts
green or red tomatoes, sliced

Make a paste of the parsley, bread crumbs, garlic, salt, and pepper, all mashed together on a plate. Heat oil and butter in a frying pan, dip tomato slices into the provencal paste, and fry the flying breaded circles on both sides.

VARIATIONS: The same procedure can be followed without fear using eggplant or zucchini, cooking the eggplant a little longer, naturellement.

SMOTHERED FLOWER
SERVES 3 or 4

conformity of
color
under cover
a vegetable
bleats
white cheese has
tumbled from someone's
pocket your mouth awaits
the word

½ head cauliflower, sliced into thin white fans
4 crookneck yellow squash, cut across or along their lengths
8 ounces tofu, drained and cut in geometrics
6 mushrooms, rinsed, patted dry, and sliced
   oil or butter
1 teaspoon sesame seeds, toasted
½ teaspoon dill weed
   meager pinch of spearmint
   white cheddar cheese

Begin steaming cauliflower, adding squash as it softens, and then tofu, cooking just barely through. Meantime, sauté mushroom slivers in oil or butter over low heat in a large frying pan for a few minutes. Once the butter is richly flavored with the memory of earth and the mushrooms are more deeply brown, stir in the steamed vegetables, and the seeds and herbs. Push around gently with wooden spatula, coating with flavor. Top with crumbled, sliced, or grated cheese, cover pan with a fitting lid, turn off heat, and stand while it sits and the cheese melts.

VARIATIONS: *Forget the cheese, and at the same point when it would come down, stir in creamed mellow white miso.*

   Serve in bowls with dill folded into yogurt or a tofu sauce.

   Leave out tofu and cheese, include miso, and break a couple of eggs directly into pan, scrambling until all holds together.

No music except this undefinable dirge manufactured in the subcellar—like a million heads of cauliflower wailing in the dark.

HENRY MILLER

STUFFED AUTUMN
SERVES 2

1 acorn squash
1 tablespoon sweet butter or sesame oil
⅛ teaspoon tumeric
¼ teaspoon cumin
⅛ teaspoon cinnamon
1 tablespoon safflower oil
1 yellow onion, chopped
1 slice of fresh ginger, minced
2 cloves garlic, minced
2 yellow crookneck squash, chopped
1 Japanese mushroom, soaked into its former plumpness in water, then sliced into spongy slivers and once again cut across
   handful of raisins or currants (optional)
   roasted squash seeds

Preheat oven to 350°. Rinse acorn squash and cut it down the middle, making two symmetrical gold bowls. Remove seeds and roast them on a cookie sheet for about 10 minutes. They may begin to dance and become their own castanets. Remove from oven to cool. Place two halves of squash, open side up, in baking pan, deposit a tablespoon of sweet butter in the hollow and along the rim of each one—or brush with sesame oil—and bake for 30 minutes while you prepare the stuffing.

Mix together tumeric, cumin and cinnamon. Sauté onion and fresh ginger in oil 4 or 5 minutes, adding garlic and the spice mixture. Add more oil if needed, the crookneck squash, mushroom pieces, and raisins. Sauté all for 5 minutes. Stuff into partly baked acorn squash halves, return to oven, and bake another 10 or 15 minutes. Sprinkle roasted seeds on top, or a shower of nothing, which is indescribably delicious.

CAESAR'S HICCUPS

   a lot of summer squash, quartered
3 cloves garlic, crushed
1 teaspoon dried basil leaves, or more fresh
   handful of parsley, finely chopped
   olive oil
   scallions, sliced (optional)
   tomatoes, chopped (optional)
   parmesan, cheddar, or sharp Italian cheese, grated
      (optional)

Steam squash until soft. Remove, toss into a bowl and mash very thoroughly with a masher, with repeated blows, until you have a pale green mush, into which the garlic is now crushed, and the basil. Stir in parsley, olive oil, and the scallions, tomatoes, cheese if they too are coming. Now it's ready to eat, unless you want to reheat in a saucepan topped with cheese so the cheese melts all over everything. Good cold, too.

THE LOST SQUASH
SERVES 2

½ cup yogurt
1 egg
1 teaspoon fennel or tarragon, chopped
1 tablespoon fresh parsley, chopped
1 teaspoon dill weed
2 tablespoons feta cheese, crumbled
2 tablespoons sharp cheddar, grated
3 zucchini, sliced or chopped
½ cup mushrooms, chopped
1 leek, sliced (or 2 scallions)
2 tomatoes, chopped

Preheat oven to 350°. Mix together yogurt, egg, herbs, and cheeses and set aside. Steam zucchini lightly with mushrooms and leek or scallion. Place in oiled casserole with chopped tomatoes and pour the sauce over all. Top it with extra cheddar. Bake until cheese is melted, 15 to 20 minutes.

the best side of me

tomatoes squashes and cauliflowers intrigue me immensely
with their lewd proposals
and their making the stability of my appetite burst
with the lust of their red yellow and white chewiness.
you're chewy, i'm looney.
i dream of soft furry things with inward claws
lodged in my brain
who open when it rains.
then whole cities built around a globe of waving squash.
we float backwards into early tickles of consciousness.
faces pull through complicated threads of greasy smiles.
my friend peter chewing on his model airplane.
the stretched frown of my tomato nanny.
if i ever walk out of this dream
my work is all over, my body releases
the captives from ten thousand labors.

ANDREI CODRESCU

SAUTÉED CONFETTI
SERVES 2

  1 **tablespoon safflower oil**
  1 **tablespoon sesame oil**
  1 **yellow onion, sliced in crescents**
  2 **scallions, sliced in thin circles**
½ **head cauliflower, cut into thin white fans**
    butternut squash, peeled and sliced
    red chard, chopped
  4 **scallions, whole**
  1 **teaspoon tamari (optional)**

Heat oil in large frying pan and sauté onion slices and concentric scallion circles into aromatic constellations. Add cauliflower and butternut squash, the golden dimension, and sauté 3 more minutes, coating every surface, sealing in the soul of each swooning fragment. Cover pan with lid and let vegetables soften with another 5 minutes or less of gentle heat. Add chard and whole scallions, toss and topple with the oil and onions and squash and cauliflower, then sprinkle with tamari, and cook another 2 minutes.

*the marvelous thing about Shakespeare
is that we can't ask him any questions*

*this beautiful man whose accents are
untouchable we gobble our own stew*

TIERRA FIRMA STEW
SERVES 4

*what is
the square
root of
silence?*

2-3 tablespoons sesame oil
  4 burdock roots (available in oriental markets), rinsed, scrubbed, scraped lightly, soaked, and cut across in 1/8" pieces, or lengthwise in matchsticks 2-3" long
1-2 carrots, sliced in thin diagonal strips or in matchsticks
  4 scallions, cut in thin translucent circles
  1 red onion, sliced
  2 summer squash, in slender slivers
  8 ounces tofu, pressed and cut in cubes
  1 tablespoon red miso, creamed in 3 tablespoons hot water
    snow peas, ends trimmed
  1 tablespoon unhulled sesame seeds, roasted in dry cast-iron frying pan

Heat oil in large frying pan and add the burdock, stirring it over moderate, then lowered, heat for 5 minutes. Add carrot slices, stir and sauté, and half the scallions and the red onion. Cook all of them over low flame for 5 more minutes. Add a bit more oil if needed and the sliced squash, tofu, and remaining scallion. Sauté another 3 minutes, pour over the creamed miso, cover, and cook gently for 5 more minutes. Add the snow peas and sprinkle with the roasted sesame seeds. Cover and cook over very low heat another few minutes.

Serve with brown rice, millet, bulghur wheat, or couscous.

KASHMIR QUICHE

Crust:

    4 tablespoons sesame oil
1½ cups whole wheat pastry flour
    1 tablespoon ground sesame seeds or gomasio
    4 tablespoons water

Preheat oven to 400°. Slowly add sesame oil to the pastry flour and sesame seeds. Add water, one tablespoon at a time, mixing with your hands until smooth. Add more water or use less, as needed. Press into oiled pie tin and bake for 15 minutes. Remove and lower oven heat to 350°.

Filling:

    2 tablespoons sesame oil
    2 onions, sliced
3-4 carrots, sliced thin
    1 green apple, chopped
    1 teaspoon tumeric
    1 teaspoon cumin
      pinch cayenne
  ¼ teaspoon ginger
  ¼ teaspoon cinnamon
  ½ teaspoon paprika
    6 ounces tofu, pressed and crumbled
    4 tablespoons tahini
    2 tablespoons water
    1 teaspoon miso
    2 ounces tofu

Heat the oil and sauté the onions, carrots, and apple with spices. Keep stirring and tossing and add the crumbled tofu. Cover and cook over low heat 15 to 20 minutes, until the vegetables are soft. Blend together tahini, water, miso, and tofu to make a sauce. Mix with vegetables and spoon all into the half-baked crust. Bake at 350° for 20 to 25 minutes.

I am thinking of the onion again, with its two O mouths, like the gaping holes in nobody. Of the outer skin, pinkish brown, peeled to reveal a greenish sphere, bald as a dead planet, glib as glass, & an odor almost animal. I consider its ability to draw tears, its capacity for self-scrutiny, flaying itself away, layer on layer, in search of its heart which is simply another region of skin, but deeper & greener. I remember Peer Gynt; I consider its sometimes double heart. Then I think of despair when the onion searches its soul & finds only its various skins; & I think of the dried tuft of roots leading nowhere & the parched umbilicus, lopped off in the garden. Not self-righteous like the proletarian potato, nor a siren like the apple. No show-off like the banana. But a modest, self-effacing vegetable, questioning, introspective, peeling itself away, or merely radiating halos like lake ripples. I consider it the eternal outsider, the middle child, the sad analysand of the vegetable kingdom. Glorified only in France (otherwise silent sustainer of soups & stews), unloved for itself alone—no wonder it draws our tears! Then I think again how the outer peel resembles paper, how soul & skin merge into one, how each peeling strips bare a heart which in turn turns skin . . .

ERICA JONG

SPINACH ACROPOLIS

SERVES 3 or 4

1 bunch green onions, chopped
¼ cup olive oil
2 bunches spinach
2 cloves garlic, minced
2 tablespoons dill weed
   parsley, chopped
¼ cup tomato sauce
1 cup cooked long-grain brown or basmatti rice
½ cup feta cheese, crumbled

Sauté the onions in oil and add the remaining ingredients except the rice and cheese. Cook until the spinach is wilted. At that sad point, when the leaves are flagging, add the rice, and cook another 5 to 10 minutes. Remove from stove and add the feta cheese to the top, cover pan and set aside for 20 minutes, or until the cheese has melted. Stir no more.

VARIATIONS: Replace rice with couscous or millet.
   Omit tomato sauce or use fresh chopped tomatoes.

UPROOTED

a whole celery root (celeriac), scraped clean and chopped in
   mouthsize pieces
fresh parsley, finely chopped
lemon
butter or oil (olive, safflower)

Steam chopped celery root until it begins to soften. Toss with lots of chopped parsley, lemon juice, and butter or oil.

Or marinate the cooked celery root in oil, lemon juice, and parsley for several hours or overnight, and eat cold on a bed of lettuce, with tabouli, olives, and other solemnities. Or mash and spread on warm pita bread.

TOFU KIMA

SERVES 2

    1 onion, chopped
    2 tablespoons safflower oil or ghee
    1 clove garlic, minced
  ½ teaspoon cumin
  ½ teaspoon tumeric
  ½ teaspoon ginger
    pinch of cayenne
2-3 potatoes, chopped
    8 ounces tofu, pressed and cubed
    1 cup fresh shelled peas
  ¼ cup hot water
    1 tomato, chopped

Sauté onion in oil or ghee until golden and add garlic and spices, stirring for 1 or 2 minutes. Enter the potatoes to cook for 5 minutes, or until they begin to brown. Now the tofu, peas, water, and tomato join the crowd, in a covered and simmering situation. Cook 15 or 20 minutes until potatoes are done.

VARIATIONS: *Use cooked white or lima beans or lentils instead of tofu.*
    Add pieces of solid white fish with the peas and tomato.

POTATO

Mysterious murky
Face of earth

He speaks
With midnight fingers
The language of eternal noon

He sprouts
With unexpected dawns
In his larder of memories

All because
In his heart
The sun sleeps

VASKO POPA

THE INORDINATE SPUD

Preheat oven to 450°. Wash and scrub a baking potato, pop into oven, prick with fork halfway through, and remove after 40 minutes. Break open and spread with grated raw milk cheddar cheese and sautéed mushrooms and chives, return to oven for another 5 to 10 minutes, remove again, and heap with chopped parsley, a little sesame oil, alfalfa or other sprouts, and yogurt. This could pass for a complete meal.

SUNFLOWER SWEET POTATOES

       sweet potatoes
       sunflower seeds
       butter
1-2 tablespoons orange juice (fresh if possible) per potato

Bake whole sweet potatoes in 425° oven about 45 minutes. Halfway through, prick their skins to let the steam spirits escape. When the potatoes are soft and you are hungry, slit them and add a little butter and a handful of sunflower seeds. Mix with the sweetness of that flesh, and then squeeze or stir in the orange juice.

DISTANT WONDER

2 tablespoons sesame oil or ghee
2 teaspoons or more of curry powder
1 onion, chopped
1 clove of garlic, minced
   banana squash, sliced and skinned
   carrots, sliced thinly on diagonal
2-3 ounces of cheddar or mozzarella cheese, grated
   cayenne

Heat oil or ghee in frying pan and fry the curry powder quickly over low heat, being careful not to burn it. Add onion and garlic, saute 5 minutes, and then welcome the vegetables, stirring to coat them with the spices. Add ½ cup of water or less depending on amount of squash and carrots, cover, and let vegetables steam to semi-softness. Add cheese, sprinkle cayenne on the cheese, replace cover, and let it all sit until the cheese has melted. Serve with a rain of parsley or chopped nuts.

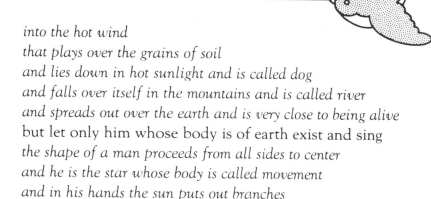

into the hot wind
that plays over the grains of soil
and lies down in hot sunlight and is called dog
and falls over itself in the mountains and is called river
and spreads out over the earth and is very close to being alive
but let only him whose body is of earth exist and sing
the shape of a man proceeds from all sides to center
and he is the star whose body is called movement
and in his hands the sun puts out branches
leaves and petals break out of silver
the corn is eaten, the animal howls, the sun flowers.

ROBERT KELLY

SALADS

PICNIC OF ESCONDIDO
avocado in a harvest
of green

several ripe avocadoes, sliced
jicama or water chestnuts, sliced thin
green peas, shelled or snow
olives
several sprigs of watercress
escarole, or another leafy lettuce

Mix with this dressing:

sesame oil
lemon juice
1 clove garlic, crushed
1 teaspoon chili powder
dash of kelp, cayenne, oregano
finely chopped parsley

Aunt Lettuce, I want to look under your skirt.

CHARLES SIMIC

COLUMBINE'S COMBINATION

dark green lettuce—anything with more soul than iceberg
cucumbers, sliced
carrots, grated
tomatoes
alfalfa or other sprouts—lentil, garbanzo, fenugreek
zucchini, sliced
radishes
sharp white cheddar or goat's cheese

Mix with this dressing:

2 **tablespoons sesame oil**
1 **teaspoon tamari**
1 **teaspoon cumin**
1 **teaspoon basil**
   juice of 1 lemon and 1 orange or juice of 2 lemons
2 **cloves garlic, crushed**

EL TOPO
the mole's lunch

>   **carrot, grated**
>   **mung bean sprouts**
>   **handful of parsley, chopped**

Toss together, or sprinkle parsley over two little heaps, and add the following dressing:

>   ½ **cup sesame oil or half sesame, half safflower**
>   **juice of two lemons**
>   ½ **teaspoon basil**
>   **garlic**

Blend, pour over salad, then top everything with a couple of tablespoons of finely ground sesame seeds.

VARIATION: Add yogurt, on top or mixed into.

SATYR'S SALAD

>   **cherry tomatoes, halved or**
>   **large tomatoes, chopped**
>   **cucumber, Armenian preferably, cut in cubes**
>   4 **ounces feta cheese**
>   **handful of parsley, chopped**
>   **greek or spiced olives**
>   3 **tablespoons olive oil**
>   **vinegar or lemon juice**
>   ¼ **teaspoon dry mustard**
>   **pinch of basil, rosemary**
>   **juice from olive jar**

Mix everything together and marinate for several hours. This salad is a meal in itself, and can also be spread over leaves of romaine.

VARIATION: Include artichoke hearts.
   Stuff into warm pita bread or a chapatti along with grains like rice or millet.

Once there was a witch's garden
more beautiful than Eve's
with carrots growing like little fish,
with many tomatoes rich as frogs,
onions as ingrown as hearts,
the squash singing like a dolphin
and one patch given over wholly to magic—
rampion, a kind of salad root,
a kind of harebell more potent than penicillin,
growing leaf by leaf, skin by skin,
as rapt and as fluid as Isadora Duncan.

ANNE SEXTON

SALADE STENDHAL

> many cherry tomatoes, halved, or several large tomatoes,
>   sliced
> 1 onion, chopped (optional)
> 1 bunch parsley, chopped fine
> many black olives

Immerse these vegetables in a delicious dressing composed of the following:

> 2 tablespoons olive oil
>   juice of 2 lemons
> ¼ teaspoon tumeric
> 1 teaspoon cumin
> ½ teaspoon honey

Marinate for an hour or two before serving.

A COLORFUL MEMORY

I remember the day of the tomatoes—how they took me unawares as I walked the neighborhood street in Athens, and happened to glance to the right, downhill on one of those side-streets in Gizi that seem so bland and so eternal: dazzling, piled neatly in the merchants' carts, orange, the orange of kumbaloy beads that seem to glow from within, the way the sun would surely look if it were not so remote and so intimidating, if it were something you could expect to eat, truly the fruit of the earth, yet here in the heart of the city, glowing like the heart of the street below, and of course I turned and followed that wonder to find the wednesday market overflowing along the next parallel street down the hill—not only tomatoes, but squash, eggplant, and the shouts of the merchants as they competed for the attention of the shoppers, trying to be heard above the wild island music played by a cassette recorder with double speakers which a beggar carried down the center of the street outspread for all to hear, as if he were carrying the torah.

I forget where I was going that day—I know I got there, and finished what I set out to do, but it is the tomatoes I remember, that miraculous vision seen as I walked unsuspecting toward some tedious goal.

JONATHAN CHAVES

TABOULI

*a salad of grains from the Middle East made light and refreshing
with lemon juice, mint, and cold*

SERVES 4 to 6

- 2 **cups cooked bulghur wheat**
- 2 **cups cooked millet**
- 3 **tablespoons olive oil**
- **juice of 3 lemons**
- 3 **cloves garlic, minced**
- **olive juice**
- ½ **cup cooked white beans (optional)**
- 2 **zucchini, chopped fine (optional)**
- 10 **or more spiced olives**
- 12 **cherry tomatoes, halved (optional)**
- 2 **mint leaves, chopped**
- **handful of parsley or a whole bunch, chopped very fine**

Start with the grain at least partly chilled. Mix with olive oil with
lemon juice and garlic and a liberal amount of juice from olives.
Mix the grains in a large bowl, pour dressing over, and toss
thoroughly, including the beans and/or zucchini if they are part of
your plans. Chop olives in small pieces, throw them in with the
tomatoes and chopped mint and parsley, and you've got tabouli.
Refrigerate, serve cold with yogurt on top, or stuffed in tomatoes,
or on a bed of lettuce.

VARIATIONS: Try using other grains such as kasha, couscous, brown rice.

THE GARDEN OF SWEET SWALLOWS

a carrot-apple-raisin salad

SERVES 4 to 6

3-4 cups carrots, finely grated
2 apples, grated a little bigger and preferably green
½ cup raisins
3 tablespoons sunflower seeds
3 tablespoons hazelnuts, almonds, and/or walnuts,
    chopped
1 cup yogurt
½ teaspoon or more cinnamon
    pinch of nutmeg
1 teaspoon or more honey
3 tablespoons orange juice

Mix yogurt dressing into itself, bleeding spices through all that white and gold. In large bowl, mix carrots and company with the dressing and prepare yourself for a carnival of chewing. This will keep a day or two, and it's also a nice place for a chopped ripe banana to find itself, immersed.

Icicle-shaped carrots that through black soil
Wove away lie like flames in the sun.

GALWAY KINNELL

Artemis naked:
the soft white
        buried sprout
of the world's first
seed.

GARY SNYDER

THE FEAST OF THE
NUMINOUS SISTERS

a salad   a séance   a lunch

lots of crunchy white mung bean sprouts
cherry tomatoes, cut in half
carrots, finely grated or shredded
bell pepper, thinly sliced
handful parsley, finely chopped

Toss the above, or arrange in little mounds of visual excitement, and pour over the following dressing:

   2 tablespoons sesame oil
   1 tablespoon lemon juice
   ½-1 teaspoon curry powder
        a clove of garlic, pressed (optional)

Over the salad now sprinkle a big spoonful of ground unhulled sesame seeds, which, in combination with the sesame oil, give this a rich flavor and endearing energy.

SWALLOWS OF ALHAMBRA

2 oranges, peeled and split into sections demarcated by
   nature
1 spanish onion, sliced thinly
½ cup black olives, drained
   butter lettuce
   parsley, chopped fine
2 tablespoons red wine vinegar
3 tablespoons olive oil
1 teaspoon honey
   a few drops of fresh orange juice

Mix the last four ingredients, which comprise a dressing, and pour
over the oranges, onions, and olives. Toss with a little parsley and
marinate in refrigerator or at room temperature for several hours.
Then toss with lettuce, or lay on top of lettuce bed, sprinkled with
more parsley.

MAÇEDOINE PROVENÇAL

sliced potatoes, slightly steamed
tomatoes, diced
parsley, finely chopped
green beans, slightly steamed and cut on diagonal

Saturate in this dressing:

olive oil
lemon juice
chives, tarragon, basil
black olives, chopped
lemon rind, grated

She was now in the habit of working every day, settled in the hotel whose windows gave out on groves of whispering cypresses or, at times, sitting 'in the court of the Alhambra watching the swallows fly in and out of the crevices of the walls, bathing in the soft air filled with the fragrance of myrtle and oleander and letting the hot sun burn her face and the palms of her hands.' In the course of the sojourn at Granada the significance of her new departure in technique struck with a conviction that overwhelmed her and made her buoyant. Long concerned with the workings of the human mind, the endlessly fascinating but finally predictable reactions of personalities, she now had a new goal: description that would express "the rhythm of the visible world."

from *The Third Rose* (of Gertrude Stein)
JOHN MALCOLM BRINNIN

THE SOFT MOUNTAIN

goats climb
tongues collide
teeth rejoice

cottage cheese
scallions, sliced thin
zucchini, sliced thin
1 carrot, half grated fine, and half in delicate orange circles
snow peas, whole or cut in half
chopped almonds or cashews, roasted or raw
finely ground sesame seeds

Mix the above ingredients in a bowl and toss with this dressing:

2 tablespoons sesame oil
1 teaspoon rice wine vinegar
juice of ½ lemon
dash of cayenne
basil, curry powder or tamari to taste

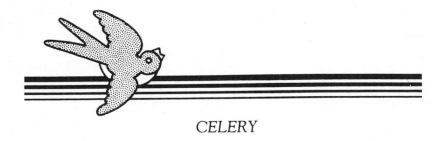

CELERY

Celery tastes tastes where in curled lashes and little bits and mostly in remains.
A green acre is so selfish and so pure and so enlivened.

GERTRUDE STEIN

ENSALADA ENSENADA

*This salad is so flavorful and such a carnival of colors that it
satisfies a hunger that is deeper than the growl of an empty day.*

The ensalada:

> **red leaf lettuce**
> **radishes, sliced**
> **red cabbage, finely sliced**
> **scallions in translucent green slivers**
> **celery**
> **bell pepper, thinly sliced**
> **tomatoes**
> **sprouts**
> **lots of fresh parsley, finely chopped**

The ensalada's red hot dressing gown:

> **2 tablespoons safflower oil**
> **3 cloves garlic, pressed**
> **1 teaspoon red vinegar**
> **juice of a lemon**
> **1 teaspoon or more chili powder**
> **avocado, blended with lemon juice, then added to
> above (optional)**

SAUCES
&
DRESSINGS

SEED YOGURT

1   **cup sesame seeds**
1   **cup sunflower seeds**
    water
    yogurt or yogurt culture

Soak the seeds in twice as much water for at least 8 hours. They can take as much of this as 24 hours at room temperature. They don't mind going through this in the refrigerator, either.

Pour seeds and soaking water into a blender and blend until very smooth, adding more water if that seems necessary.

Strain through sieve for a finer yogurt, or don't for a thicker more textured product, into a bowl or jar in any case, and stir in a couple of spoonfuls of plain yogurt or yogurt culture (or, if you've been at this a while, previously made seed yogurt).

Cover with a napkin and leave in a warm place a few hours. The longer it's cultured, the stronger it gets. If it separates, reunite it with a spoon.

VARIATIONS: *This may be made with almonds, too, or vary amounts of sesame and sunflower seeds. Some people find the sesame seeds too bitter. Pumpkin seeds can also be included.*

THE SUPREMACY OF CASHEW

*something exquisite for the top
of vegetables, pilaf, plain cooked grains*

1   **tablespoon safflower oil**
2   **tablespoons whole wheat flour, millet meal or brown
      rice flour**
2   **tablespoons raw cashew butter**
2   **tablespoons mellow white miso**
½   **cup water**

Heat oil in saucepan or frying pan, and over low heat, stir in, bit by
bit, the flour. Cream nut butter and miso together in hot water,
first a tablespoon of hot water, then another, until you have half a
cup. Slowly add this to the flour and oil mixture, which hasn't
scorched because you've been attentive, or because you've
creamed the miso and cashew butter to begin with and were ready
to perform the ceremony of completion in due time. Heat slowly,
stirring continuously, and adding more water if the sauce is still
too thick. In a matter of 2 or 3 minutes, it's ready to stick to your
brain (which is where all good food goes).

SUGGESTION: *Make a double or triple recipe, so you have some around in
moments of gastronomical ennui.*

VARIATION: *Vary the amounts of cashew butter or miso for relative saltiness
or richness.*

A SUPERMARKET IN CALIFORNIA

What thoughts I have of you tonight, Walt Whitman, for I walked down the sidestreets under the trees with a headache self-conscious looking at the full moon.

In my hungry fatigue, and shopping for images, I went into the neon fruit supermarket, dreaming of your enumerations!

What peaches and what penumbras! Whole families shopping at night! Aisles full of husbands! Wives in the avocados, babies in the tomatoes!—and you, Garcia Lorca, what were you doing down by the watermelons?

I saw you, Walt Whitman, childless, lonely old grubber, poking among the meats in the refrigerator and eyeing the grocery boys.

I heard you asking questions of each: Who killed the pork chops? What price bananas? Are you my Angel?

I wandered in and out of the brilliant stacks of cans following you, and followed in my imagination by the store detective.

We strode down the open corridors together in our solitary fancy tasting artichokes, possessing every frozen delicacy, and never passing the cashier.

Where are we going, Walt Whitman? The doors close in an hour. Which way does your beard point tonight?

(I touch your book and dream of our odyssey in the supermarket and feel absurd.)

Will we walk all night through solitary streets? The trees add shade to shade, lights out in the houses, we'll both be lonely.

Will we stroll dreaming of the lost America of love past blue automobiles in driveways, home to our silent cottage?

Ah, dear father, graybeard, lonely old courage-teacher, what America did you have when Charon quit poling his ferry and you got out on a smoking bank and stood watching the boat disappear on the black waters of Lethe?

ALLEN GINSBERG

FUNGI SURTOUT

½ **pound mushrooms, sliced**
2 **tablespoons unsalted butter, or safflower oil**
1 **cup yogurt**
½ **teaspoon dill weed**

Sauté mushrooms in butter or oil until soft and the medium has become dusky like the woods. Remove from pan and stir into a bowl with yogurt, adding dill weed. Serve on rice, tofu and vegetables, or fold into an omelet.

VARIATIONS: *Sauté a chopped onion with the mushrooms, add minced garlic, and forget the dill.*
   Squeeze half a lemon into the bowl, too.
   Add a teaspoon of tamari to sautéed mushrooms.

GUACAMOLE

several ripe avocadoes
a juicy lemon or two
1 **clove garlic, crushed**
1 **tablespoon olive oil (optional)**
½ **teaspoon onion juice, freshly squeezed**
chopped tomatoes (optional)
chili powder (optional)

Mash avocadoes with fork and add lemon juice, onion juice, garlic, and mix well. Then the rest, if there is any more.

Spread on chapattis, use as a base for other sandwiches to pile up on, dip into with tortilla chips or toasted pita bread or raw carrot sticks and jicama.

VARIATIONS: *Thin with more lemon juice and oil and use as a salad dressing.*
   Mix with yogurt for a more diffused flavor and lighter experience.

TOUCH OF TAHINI

½ cup safflower oil
¼ cup olive oil
2 tablespoons tamari

5 tablespoons tahini
¼ cup lemon juice
1 clove garlic, minced
(optional)

Mix in blender. This is a salad dressing, a dip, a sauce for steamed vegetables and grains.

THE COUNTESS OF CHERVIL

mayonnaise
safflower oil
lemons to juice

chives
chervil
scallions

Search your heart for the proportions that will matter to your taste. Blend by hand or machine and take note of the success of your guess.

IN A BLUE VEIN
bleu cheese dressing

½ cup yogurt or half yogurt/half buttermilk
2 tablespoons safflower oil
juice of 1 lemon
1 clove garlic
1-2 ounces bleu cheese

Mix in blender. Beautiful with whole leaves of romaine lettuce, or use as a spread on sandwiches with sprouts, tomatoes, more cheese, cucumber, spinach leaves.

MOUNT TOFU

2 tablespoons white miso
2 tablespoons warm water
2 tablespoons lemon juice
8 ounces tofu, crumbled
1 teaspoon sesame oil

Cream the miso in a couple of tablespoons warm water and lemon juice. Add in blender to crumbled tofu with oil and blend. Vary liquid to please your sense of density.

VARIATIONS: Add 1 shallot, chopped, or 1 tablespoon chopped onion, or a clove of garlic, minced.

Add 1 to 3 tablespoons sesame tahini, increasing amount of liquid proportionately.

Make with light yellow or red or brown rice miso, or a combination of one of these with mellow white.

Add tamari to taste.

For more texture, include a little chopped bell pepper or celery.

Add toasted sesame seeds.

The variations in proportions and ingredients are unlimited. Each time make it differently. Use tofu sauce on sandwiches, to top vegetables or grains, as a salad dressing, with artichokes, as a dip for raw vegetables. Use in place of mayonnaise, yogurt, or sour cream.

THE AWAKENING

the awakened cow

1 cup yogurt
2 tablespoons miso, creamed in 1 tablespoon lemon juice

Mix together and serve with steamed vegetables and sprouts. Use as dip for raw vegetables like carrot, jerusalem artichoke.

VARIATIONS: Add tamari.

Add a tablespoon of sesame butter or tahini.

Add crushed garlic.

THE HOT KIMONO

onion
celery
ginger, fresh minced root
whole lemon
safflower or sesame oil
vinegar (rice or cider)
tamari (take it easy)

Mix the above in a blender. This dressing has an intriguing substantial texture and a baffling, refreshing taste. It's good with a very simple salad: butter lettuce, *par exemple.*

FERNANDO'S REPLY

chopped onion
olive oil
chili powder
yogurt

Sauté onion in olive oil until soft and glazed. Stir in chili powder to taste, cooking another minute. Pour this mixture into a bowl of yogurt and watch it bleed. Spread on grains or a tostada.

VARIATIONS: *Add chopped fresh tomato either to the cooking process or to the bowl of yogurt.*

And/or add chili peppers or fresh cilantro, which could never be confused with anything else above or below the surface of the earth.

Let him contemplate Brahman as adoration, and all desires will fall down before him in adoration. Let him contemplate Brahman as the Supreme Lord, and he will be endowed with supremacy. Let him contemplate Brahman as the destructive agent, and his enemies who hate him and also those who do not hate him will perish.

This he who is in this man, and that he who is in yonder sun, both are one.

He who knows this, after dying to this world, attains the self which consists of food, attains the self which consists of the vital breath, attains th self which consists of the mind, attains the self which consists of the intellect, attains the self which consists of bliss. Then he goes up and down these worlds, eating the food he desires, assuming the forms he likes. He sits, singing the chant of the non-duality of Brahman: "Ah! Ah! Ah!"

"I am food, I am food, I am food! I am the eater of food, I am the eater of food, I am the eater of food! I am the uniter, I am the uniter, I am the uniter!

"I am the first-born of the true, prior to the gods, and the navel of Immortality. He who gives me away, he alone preserves me. He who eats food—I, as food, eat him.

"I (as the Supreme Lord) overpower the whole world. I am radiant as the sun."

Whosoever knows this (attains Liberation). Such, indeed, is the Upanishad.

from the TAITTIRIYA UPANISHAD

DRINKS,
DESSERTS
&
BREAKFASTS

THE TASTE

There is a drink which only the old ever taste. Everyone knows that the day is full of rocks, some large, some small, which move. They are all invisible and no one mentions them, but everyone knows that they are rocks. No one knows how to get past them, or to enter them, or to see what is inside them. They are said to contain the treasure of Age, which no one has ever looked on—a black treasure.

At night when only the old are awake, black springs rise in some of the rocks and begin to flow toward some of the old. The slow streams seldom choose for destinations the old who are nearest to them. The rocks in which they rise have all moved. The withered body toward which a stream starts to make its way may have passed the source years before and not have known it. How wide the world is now! How empty! How far a stream may have to flow! Meanwhile the old are dying.

As a stream passes through the dark meadows, birds that are standing there turn to look. Each time they think it is Memory once more. But is is not Memory. Each of the birds was a color, once, and this is where they go.

When at last a stream lies on the tongue it set out for, it rests. There is a moment of trembling. Tears come out and sit in the night. After a while the stream gets up and goes to its boat and loads the old person into it and they drift away together toward the valley. In the morning the body that has been visited can no longer stand, no longer speak. It swallows and swallows as though trying to remember tasting water for the first time.

W.S. MERWIN

ℋℰℛℬ ᴛℰᴀ ᴄᴏℒᴅ ᴅℛℐℕℋᔕ

a clear message
drink a glass of water

lemon grass
fresh ginger root
Boil ginger root three minutes, add lemon grass and steep. Chill
and ice.

hibiscus
lemon grass
spearmint
lemon juice
orange juice
Steep the first three for 5 minutes; add juices and chill.

2 slices chinese licorice
2 sticks cinnamon
2 slices fresh ginger
Boil 15 minutes or longer. Serve hot or cold.

Sing your iridescent thirst.

RENE CHAR

I make poems which I recite to myself, which I taste, which I play with. I feel no need to communicate them to anyone, even to people I like a lot. I don't write them down. It's so good to daydream, to stammer around something which remains a secret for oneself. It's a sin of gluttony.

BLAISE CENDRARS

MOUND OF VENUS
an interplanetary sundae
SERVES 1 or 2

8 ounces plain yogurt
1 teaspoon vanilla
¼ cup pistachios, ground

Transubstantiate the yogurt with the vanilla, watching the white soften into gold. Now mix in the ground but not pulverized pistachios, and place the heavenly mixture in a freezer for not more than an hour. When it's ready to eat, you will be too.

PANAMANIAN MOON

bananas
honey
lemon juice
butter
almonds, chopped

Preheat oven to 350°. Slice the bananas in half and place on a big piece of foil. Drizzle the bananas with honey, a few drops of lemon juice, and dot with butter: *noisettes de beurre.* Sprinkle with chopped almonds, wrap in foil, and bake for 15 minutes.

VARIATION: For a "Puerto Rican Moon," add some rum to the sequence above.

GAUGUIN'S JULEP

    2 **papayas**
    4 **sweet juicy valencia oranges**
 1-2 **limes**
       maybe yogurt

Blend papaya and oranges in blender, with lime juice, pour into
cups or bowls and eat or drink. Or save part of the papaya whole,
cut in little pieces and add to tropical slush in a bowl and top with
yogurt.

THE PAPAYAN CIVILIZATION
banana cream hawaiian papayan sundae

bananas
raw plain kefir
applesauce (optional)

This is a tropical fruit soup. Blend ripe bananas in a blender with
raw plain kefir and some applesauce, which adds a tartness that
the shamelessly cloying banana could well learn a few things from.

Now you have a kefir shake to shrink from, or to drink. Better yet,
you have a sauce to pour over sliced bananas and papaya.

VARIATION: *Use papaya instead of banana in the kefir.*
  Mix banana, papaya, or both, with kefir.

THE WELL

The well! . . . Platero, how deep, how dark-green, how fresh, how resonant this word is! It seems as if it were the word itself that pierces, gyrating, the dark earth until it reaches the cold water.

Look; the fig tree ornaments and destroys the edges. Inside, within reach, between bricks with moss, a blue flower of penetrating smell has just opened. A swallow has, lower down, her nest. Then, beyond a porch of dead shadows there is an emerald palace, and a lake, which, when a stone is thrown against its peace, gets angry and growls. And at last, the sky.

(Night comes and the moon shines down there in the bottom, decked with fickle stars. Silence! Along the paths life has gone far away. Down the well the soul flees to the depths. One can see through it the other side of the twilight. And it looks as if from its mouth the giant of the night, master of all the world's secrets, were about to come out. Oh, quiet and magic labyrinth, shady and fragrant park, magnetic, enchanted hall!)

"Platero, if one day I throw myself into this well, it will not be, believe me, to kill myself, but to catch the stars more quickly."

Platero brays, thirsty and wistful. From the well comes a swallow, frightened, confused and silent.

JUAN RAMÓN JIMENEZ

SWEET DREAMS
SERVES 4

2 **cups butternut squash, chopped and steamed**
3 **apples, chopped and steamed**
1 **cup whole wheat pastry flour**
½ **cup brown rice flour or rice cream**
1 **teaspoon cinnamon**
2 **tablespoons tahini**

Preheat oven to 350°. Stir together the flours and cinnamon and set aside. Mash steamed squash and apple in another bowl, reserving some of the apple pieces whole, to spread their concentrated sweetness into the cookies to come, mystery in the center of the dough.

Stir flour mixture into squash-apple mash, add tahini and some water if the dough is too stiff.

Form into any flattened shape you want—about the size of a teaspoon's dream—squeezing the dough through your hands. Place on cookie sheets oiled with safflower or sesame oil and bake for about 15 minutes—not too long, or these little darlings will lose their soft centers, their yielding flesh. They are best so, plunged into with admiring teeth.

BERNARD'S BIRTHDAY
a carrot cake with rice bran syrup

  1 **cup safflower oil**
  3 **eggs**
  ½ **cup rice bran syrup**
  2 **cups whole wheat pastry flour**
1½ **teaspoons cinnamon**
1½ **teaspoons allspice**
  ¼ **teaspoon cloves**
  ⅛ **teaspoon nutmeg**
2½ **teaspoons vanilla**
  2 **cups grated carrot**
  ¼ **cup chopped nuts**

Preheat oven to 325°. Mix ingredients by hand in order given and pour into greased flat cake pan. Bake for 40 minutes, or until knife plunged into center comes out naked. Frost with cream cheese whipped with orange peel, orange juice, and a little honey.

APPLE—*for Pablo Neruda*

Apple
I cannot spell
The juice of your life
Into this poem
I want to
I want beautiful
Women
In Spanish shoes
Biting my cheeks out
And spitting
The core of me
Into the high arena
Of poems
Or by fruit stands

In pink cities
Under a wax sky
That melts
With every syllable
Bouncing red
Off my hips

Forgive me, apple
I want desk girls
In thin blouses
Warming their ovaries
Over the possibility
Of magic
Exceeding even
Television and
Broiler ovens
And baked apples
In cream
I want insects

Fainting in my presence

Apple
You have fed
Movie queens
And a hundred Buddhas
And Adams
How many gangsters
On holiday
Have feasted
On your blood?
What poet
Sinks into the world
The way
A preacher does into you
On hot Sundays
At the Baptismal picnic
In sweet Alabama
God in his sweat
And your white juice
In his mouth?

Apple, I know
this jealousy
Pushes the clock back
To Creation
How I want
A round
Fat
World of words
As when I had
All my ribs
And women

HAROLD SCHNEIDER

PINK CITIES UNDER WAX SKIES
an apple dessert

1   cup whole wheat pastry flour
1   teaspoon cinnamon
6   tablespoons sweet butter
2   tablespoons rice bran syrup or maple syrup
3   rome beauty or pippin apples, sliced thin and sprinkled
    sparingly with lemon juice

Preheat oven to 350°. In mixing bowl, toss flour with half of the cinnamon and cut in 5 tablespoons of butter. Abandon your implements and dive in with your hands, adding the syrup and squeezing the dough through your fingers.

Oil an ample baking dish and crumble a thin layer of dough on the bottom. Top with apples tossed with remaining cinnamon and dotted with the remaining sweet butter. Add another layer of the syrup dough, crumbled through your fingers and rained down upon the rosy sliced fruit. Bake for about half an hour.

A SUPERIOR TREAT

1 tablespoon oil or butter
2 tablespoons whole wheat flour, millet meal, or brown
   rice flour
3 tablespoons raw cashew butter
1-2 tablespoons Yinnies rice syrup
½ cup water
   cinnamon (optional)

In saucepan or frying pan, heat oil or butter and stir in flour a little at a time over very low heat, being cautious about the imminent danger of scorching. Turn off heat. Mix cashew butter and rice syrup and cinnamon, adding hot water a little at a time until you have half a cup. Turn heat back on, very low, and add the nut-syrup gradually to the thickening agent beneath. Barely simmer until a gorgeous consistency has appeared and prepare your tongue for a plausible orgy of restraint. Delicious at breakfast with mixed grains, cooked millet, oatmeal (especially scotch oats which are slightly caramel by nature), or cream of wheat.

VARIATION: *Add a little vanilla with water.*

*Whenever she cooked dinner she kept
her apron pockets stuffed with caramels
made from little sayings of Emily Dickinson.*

SAINT JOHN'S SUCKER

These amounts are approximate and can be improvised until the right consistency and taste concur.

    1 **cup nut butter (almond butter, raw or roasted, sesame peanut butter, peanut butter)**
    ¼ **cup rice bran syrup**
    ¼ **cup dry milk powder (fine powder available from health food store, not boxed, granulated kind)**
    1 **teaspoon vanilla**
    2 **tablespoons carob powder (St. John's Bread)**
    1 **teaspoon cinnamon (optional)**
       chopped brazil nuts, filberts, almonds

Mix in order given, with your hands. Lick them often to see how the taste is coming along. Sift carob to break up its tendency to stick to itself, forcing through sieve with back of spoon. Vary amount of milk powder until the mixture is easy to form into a cylinder, which you then wrap in waxed paper, refrigerate, and whack off in slices of pleasure. Tastes like fudge and feels like food.

THE SILKEN TENT

an arrival
fragrant
with desire

SERVES 4

2 cups pear juice
3 cups water
1 cup millet, ground
½ cup couscous, ground
2 tablespoons apricot oil
½-1 teaspoon cinnamon
½ cup whole couscous

Bring water and pear juice to boil in saucepan, and slowly, very slowly, pour in the ground millet, stirring and not worrying if lumps form. When it's all there, turn down heat, add ground couscous, apricot oil, and cinnamon, and cover and cook over low flame for about 15 minutes, until half of liquid is absorbed. Then add the whole couscous, recover, and steam another 5 to 10 minutes, stirring once or twice.

VARIATIONS: During the last 5 minutes of steaming, add a tablespoon of mellow white miso and mix thoroughly into the grains.

Make cakes by forming balls and rolling in ground pistachio nuts.

Make chapattis by mixing with whole wheat pastry flour, water if needed or more pear juice, and small pieces of pear. Cook like pancakes on ungreased griddle or in cast-iron frying pan until crisp on outside and soft and sweet within.

Roll into balls with cashew or almond butter. Add Yinnies rice syrup for a stickier, sweeter experience.

STUDY OF TWO PEARS

I

Opusculum paedagogum.
The pears are not viols,
Nudes or bottles.
They resemble nothing else.

II

They are yellow forms
Composed of curves
Bulging toward the base.
They are touched red.

III

They are not flat surfaces
Having curved outlines.
They are round
Tapering toward the top.

IV

In the way they are modeled
There are bits of blue.
A hard dry leaf hangs
From the stem.

V

The yellow glistens.
It glistens with various yellows,
Citrons, oranges and greens
Flowering over the skin.

VI

The shadows of the pears
Are blobs on the green cloth.
The pears are not seen
As the observer wills.

WALLACE STEVENS

SONG OF THE BARREN ORANGE TREE

Woodcutter.
Cut my shadow from me.
Free me from the torment
of seeing myself without fruit.

Why was I born among mirrors?
The day walks in circles around me,
and the night copies me
in all its stars.

I want to live without seeing myself.
And I will dream that ants
and thistleburrs are my
leaves and my birds.

Woodcutter.
Cut my shadow from me.
Free me from the torment
of seeing myself without fruit.

FEDERICO GARCÍA LORCA

ROCKY RICOTTA

1 cup ricotta cheese
3 tablespoons honey
   finely chopped almonds (roasted or raw)
1 teaspoon finely grated fresh orange peel
   sprinkle or two of cinnamon

Mix in a bowl and spread on toast, pita, rye crackers, English muffins, or any other solid background. Smear on apple slices. Add raisins. Eat the shaved orange.

JANE EYRE OATMEAL CAKE

This is really a big oatmeal cookie
SERVES 4

   1 stick unsalted butter
½-2/3 cup honey
   1 egg
   1 teaspoon vanilla
   1 cup whole wheat pastry flour
   1 teaspoon baking powder
   1 cup oats
   ½ cup raisins
  2/3 cup nuts

Preheat oven to 325°. Cream butter, adding egg, honey and vanilla once butter is malleable and receptive. Mix dry ingredients together and stir in thoroughly with spoon or electric mixer.

On a greased cookie sheet, place this oatmeal mixture in the resemblance of one cookie with giant intentions. Bake until golden in color and chewy to the touch.

THE MUSE OF OATS
a Swiss and familiar breakfast

raw rolled oats, soaked in milk to cover
shredded green apples
ground hazelnuts
chopped oranges, bananas, peaches, or any other fruit
raisins
yogurt (optional)
honey (optional)
pear or apple juice (optional)

After oats have soaked for a couple of hours, add nuts, fruit and raisins. Serve with yogurt and honey if you want it sweeter, or instead of honey, stir in pear or apple juice.

JENITA'S MORNING RAGA
whole grain pancakes

1¼ cup ground whole wheat berries
½-¾ cup ground millet
    dash cinnamon
¼ teaspoon salt
2 tablespoons safflower oil

Mix ground wheat and millet, cinnamon and salt in bowl; add enough water, with oil, to bring on a consistency of heavy cream, or less if you want to have very thick, chewy pancakes. Cook like any pancakes on a hot cast iron skillet or griddle, that is, turning when bubbles appear on top.

Serve with rice syrup and butter, with maple syrup, "Rocky Ricotta," sliced strawberries and yogurt, to name just a few possible embellishments. These are also good cold with cashew, almond, or peanut butter, tahini, or a miso spread.

THE DAWN OF CHAPPO
SERVES 2

1 **cup rolled oats or 1 cup scotch oats**
2 **cups water**
   rice bran syrup
   cinnamon
   sesame seeds, ground
   hazelnuts, chopped

Cook oatmeal in water over very low heat 20 to 25 minutes. You may add a little rice bran syrup and cinnamon during the cooking, and definitely later. Serve with milk, rice bran syrup, seeds, cinnamon, and hazelnuts.

VARIATIONS: Use ½ cup millet, ½ cup scotch oats, and cook half an hour.
  Add fresh wheat germ.
  Serve with "A Superior Treat" sauce.
  Serve with maple instead of rice bran syrup.
  Include raisins, apple fragments, bananas, during the cooking or at the end, which is the beginning.

LES PÊCHES DE NUIT

peaches
cinnamon
nutmeg

Gently cook a saucepan of peaches for a couple of hours, while they make their own syrup out of such heat, such passions of fructose. Add cinnamon, a little nutmeg too maybe, and keep this elixir around for yogurt sundaes—peaches, spiced, the syrup, yogurt, ground almonds and cashews, a few slices of sun-sweetened orange.

Like the sensitive tip of the tongue at the height of its enjoyment, if this tip of the tongue became instantaneously a big, fat pink hippopotamus replete with that enjoyment, and not only one, but a hundred big-bellied hippos, and ten thousand sows, suckling already biggish little pigs snuggling against their swollen flanks, and all this huddled together one against the other, and if the height of the enjoyment thus spread out and multiplied were solely the fact of being pink, pink, pink, stupidly, deliriously, paradisiacally pink, pink enough to make you howl,—unless you had the soul of a whore and took a flabby pleasure in yielding to it,—that was the way I was seeing pink. I was up to my eyes in pink, pink besieged me, licked me, wanted to confound me with itself. But I refused to fall for it. I'd have been ashamed.

HENRI MICHAUX

THE GORGEOUS PLATITUDE
a strawberry shortcake without its pants
SERVES 3 or 4

  2 **cups strawberries**
  1 **cup plain yogurt**
  1 **tablespoon strawberry kefir (optional)**
 ½ **teaspoon cinnamon**
  1 **teaspoon vanilla**
     toasted slivered almonds

Find some gorgeous strawberries and bring them home. Cut them
as you would for some royal family, or a wayfarer navigating by
his broken heart. Stir the glistening fruit into a bowl of plain
yogurt, add the strawberry kefir, some cinnamon, and vanilla, and
consider the company of almonds—and one big strawberry on
top.

LE GÂTEAU IVRE

a peach-banana nut cake

SERVES 4 to 6

  1 **cup whole wheat flour**
  1 **cup unbleached flour**
  1 **teaspoon baking powder**
  1 **teaspoon baking soda**
    pinch of sea salt
 ½ **cup brown sugar**
 ½ **cup honey**
  1 **cup oil**
  2 **eggs, well-beaten**
2/3 **cup milk**
  1 **teaspoon vanilla**
  8 **dried peaches, sliced and moistened in water**
 ½ **cup almonds, cut in half**
 ½ **cup raisins**
  3 **ripe bananas**
 ½ **cup dried papaya or other dried fruit**
 ¼ **cup sliced prunes**

Preheat oven to 350°. Sift flours, baking powder, baking soda, and salt together four times and set aside. Blend together the sugar, honey, and oil. Add the eggs, milk, and vanilla. Mix together the fruits and nuts. Add the fruit mixture to the dry mixture, adding liquid alternately and stirring with each addition.

Pour into greased cake pan and bake for 35-40 minutes or until golden brown. A toothpick will come out looking pretty clean.

BLUE MOON SOUP

    blueberries
    and
    yogurt

NIRVANA

Is it to sit
beneath a peach
with will akimbo,
divining flesh
from skin to pit,
but not to reach
beyond the blush
to mitigate the limbo?

PAUL AAEN

the time for our journey
is the ultimate flight
of the mind

APPENDIX

ABOUT MISO

An attempted interview with miso:

Q: "Who are you, anyway?"

A: "I've been through so many changes since I was a soybean that I find your question perplexing, cruel, and in bad taste."

Miso, a paste made from soybeans, sometimes grains (barley, brown rice), and salt, and fermented by special enzyme action, appears repeatedly in this book. It comes in so various a range of species that you would do well to have several kinds available, the better to taste the difference. There are dark, rich or heavy misos and lighter, more delicate, even sweet ones, though they are all salty to some degree. Miso is usually added toward the end of cooking to avoid boiling it, as too much heat destroys the lactobacillus bacteria which like to live in the intestines and help out in the lower levels of digestion—which is one reason for having a cup of miso soup as the beginning of a meal. Another reason is that miso contains all eight of the essential amino acids, completing for other proteins what they need to be embraced and utilized by your body. Miso's contribution of vitamin B12 is essential to a vegetarian diet; this remarkable food is generally strengthening and energizing as well as flavorful.

Miso is good in sauces, dressings, soups, stews, grain dishes, and spreads. To use it in any of these, cream it first: spoon the miso into a small bowl or cup, and add a tablespoon of hot water or stock, stir, add another spoonful of liquid, and maybe another, until the miso is evenly taken into this more fluid form. Now it's ready to be received into a larger world.

WHAT TO DO WITH TOFU

Tofu, a curd made from soybeans, happens in many of these pages. Not too complex or astonishing in taste by itself, it accommodates itself admirably with other foods and flavors. Tofu, like many things in the known world, comes in two basic guises: soft and hard, relative terms, to each other, and not to a rock or a breast. Soft tofu is the one for sauces and dressings; the more solid, dense form is sautéed with vegetables, dropped into soups, dried and crumbled over salads, bubbled in stews.

Many stores, even super ones, carry tofu; health food stores and Japanese markets certainly do. It comes vacuum packed or in tubs, suspended in water, which you must drain when you bring it home and replace with fresh water, changing once a day for as long as you keep the tofu in your refrigerator.

When you are ready to use the tofu, drain it in a colander and then press it, to remove more excess moisture: cut the curd into whatever shape and size you want, and wrap in a dish towel or paper towels, which can now, resting on a counter or a plate, absorb the water, and solidify the substance. To speed the process, you can place the wrapped tofu on a plate, and use another plate, with a rock or other heavy object as a weight on top, to give the squeeze a little encouragement.

Tofu is versatile, cheap, high in protein, low in calories. It can be used as a stand-in for cheese, meat, pasta, oil, in many wonderful ways. Once you've become familiar with it, it will become a thing with its own reality, and will replace only itself.

ABOUT SEAWEED

Among the edible lives of the ocean are many seaweeds, high in iodine and trace minerals and unusual in taste and texture. Wakame, hijiki, dulse, kombu, and nori are some of the more commonly used vegetables of the sea, available in health food stores and Japanese markets. Before using, soak in water for 15 minutes if you're planning to cook the seaweed with other foods, as in "Miso Soup" and "The Mud Pie Mistake." Hijiki, delicate black strands of sealife, can be used in salads after soaking. Wakame and kombu are both used in soups. Nori is stuffed for sushi. Dulse is powdered like kelp as a condiment, or the leaves are eaten raw or cooked.

SUGAR

A violent luck and a whole sample and even then quiet.

A mind under is exact and so it is necessary to have a mouth and eye glasses.

A question of sudden rises and more time than awfulness is so easy and shady. There is precisely that noise . . . .

GERTRUDE STEIN

GLOSSARY

*A swallow's garden of
curious words*

Burdock See "Tierra Firma Stew" for how to handle this root. Almost mythical properties are attributed to this friend from the earth.

Carob Also known as St. John's Bread, for John the Baptist survived on the sustaining properties of the pod from the carob tree during his days in the wilderness. Available as a powder, carob tastes similar to chocolate, and is used in drinks, in baking, in candies.

Chapatti A very flat, unleavened bread, the bread of India, Hunza, and Nepal. Most health food stores have packaged chapattis made of whole wheat, barley and millet flour; you can also make your own. See recipe.

Ghee Clarified butter, used in Indian cooking, made by heating butter over a low flame and patiently and repeatedly scraping off the whiteness that floats to the top with a spoon. What's left is ghee, a less cholesterol-saturated substance which will keep for weeks unrefrigerated. Store it in a jar. Ghee has a very distinct flavor and can be used both in cooking and to put on top of things, like vegetables, pilaf, chapattis, breakfast cereal.

Gomasio A condiment which comes out of combining salt and ground sesame seeds. First they are dry-roasted in a cast iron frying pan together, and then ground in a suribachi (a specially textured bowl with wooden pestle for crushing the seeds) or in a blender. The proportion of salt to sesame seeds can vary, but use much less salt.

Kelp powder A seasoning to replace salt, made from kelp seaweed, and very high in iodine and other minerals.

Kuzu A root, available as a powder similar to arrowroot, with nutritional and thickening properties.

Miso   A fermented soybean paste which comes in many varieties and tastes, all somewhat salty; valuable both for protein and flavor as well as digestion. See "About Miso."

Pita   Also called pocket bread. An Arabic open shell of whole wheat to stuff with whatever you want. Very tasty toasted. Pita comes plain or with sesame seeds.

Ramen   A light eggless Oriental noodle; whole wheat ramen is accessible in health food stores.

Soba   Another noodle, usually made from whole wheat and buckwheat flours.

Sweets   Rice bran syrup and "Yinnies" rice syrup are both available at health food stores, and are sweeteners with food value as well as flavor. Rice bran is especially high in niacin, other B vitamins, minerals. Maple syrup, honey, and molasses also have something over sugar, a noted absence in this book.

Tahini   A paste or butter made from sesame seeds, a rich and flavorful substance used extensively in the Middle East and in this book. Sesame seed is an excellent source of protein and calcium, and tahini is a spreadable and mixable form in which to ingest the seed.

Tamari   A kind of soy sauce, or shoyu, with a dark and pronounced and salty flavor. Use sparingly so as not to overwhelm.

Tofu   A curd from soybeans, a versatile protein, a pale cube. See "What To Do With Tofu."

GRAINS

Grain and Man: fraternal twins in the womb of time

Grain is seed. As seed, it holds the promise, the wisdom, the ontology of the plant. To chew that seed is to be imbued with that tiny explosion. We transmute as our cells echo the musical notes of mastication, the genetic script of the seed.

Barley The guy in the soup, embracing the stem of a mushroom, swimming like a lost pearl in the cry of the ocean.

Buckwheat Toasted, becoming kasha, becoming Russia, hard and cold. Disappears in the mouth and surfaces in the brain, warming the thoughts, hands, feet, face. A dark energy, tugging with the earth.

Corn Ah, so sweet. Mayan maize. Resident of tortilla, hero of mamaliga, Rumanian opera star, an ear is listening to these words.

Millet Despair of "The Seven Samurai," an unknown wonder. Miraculous dimensions of energy are packed into such a tiny golden sphere. Ask any caged bird. Radiant with protein, alkaline in attitude, millet knows the body, takes it in.

Oats Relegated to the breakfast table, the trough, and the cookie jar, steel cut, Scotch, and rolled. Combine with other grains also in cereals, breads, desserts.

Rice Long-grain and short-grain brown rice, naturally white Basmatti rice, wild rice, rice flour and bran. Eat it naked, unadorned, eat it often, releasing its precious secrets. Dynamite of the gods. Gyrations of vitamins, flavor of fuel.

Wheat We think we know it, but we have only begun to explore the possibilities of all its forms: wheat grass, cracked wheat, semolina, bulghur wheat, whole wheat berries, and the ubiquitous flour in breads, chapattis, noodles, pancakes, cookies, crusts. And in Africa, couscous, each grain a soufflé, a chewy balloon.

ODE TO SALT

I saw the salt
in this shaker
in the salt flats.
I know
you
will never believe me,
but
it sings,
the salt sings, the hide
of the salt plains,
it sings
through a mouth smothered
by earth.
I shuddered in those deep
solitudes
when I heard
the voice
of
the salt
in the desert.
Near Antofagasta
the entire
salt plain
speaks:
it is a
broken
voice,
a song full
of grief.
Then in its own mines
rock salt, a mountain
of buried light,
a cathedral through which
   light passes,

crystal of the sea, abandoned
by the waves.
And then on every table
on this earth,
salt,
your nimble
body
pouring out
the vigorous light
over
our foods.
Preserver
of the stores
of the ancient ships,
you were
an explorer
in the ocean,
substance
going first
over the unknown, barely open
routes of the sea-foam.
Dust of the sea, the tongue
receives a kiss
of the night sea from you:
taste recognizes
the ocean in each salted morsel,
and therefore the smallest,
the tiniest
wave of the shaker
brings home to us
not only your domestic whiteness
but the inward flavor of the infinite.

PABLO NERUDA

PERMISSIONS

Nothing I cared, in the lamb white days, that time would take me
Up to the swallow thronged loft by the shadow of my hand,
   In the moon that is always rising,
      Nor that riding to sleep
   I should hear him fly with the high fields
And wake to the farm forever fled from the childless land.
Oh as I was young and easy in the mercy of his means,
      Time held me green and dying
   Though I sang in my chains like the sea.

DYLAN THOMAS

AFTERWORD

I did not so much write this book as I was swallowed by it, as it engulfed, in fragments, my thoughts, my habits, my spine . . .

Given the chance or the challenge, the charge or obligation to be, I submit to my own acts of creation as a way of extending and compressing this time, substance, this itch. That is what makes me feel alive and notice that anything else is. And food has to shove its way into this picture as well as poetry—it's not enough to chew, blink, ingest: it has to have rhythm, sound, magic, it has to connect me to this and other worlds. Taste being what it is—good or bad, bittersweet, succulent, monstrous, cloying, satisfied or perverse—there are other senses involved in any semblance of necessity or pleasure, and it is to these, too, that this book addresses itself, these senses which are twitching in you.

Because the recipes accumulated during metamorphoses I no longer care to recount, taciturnity being one of the later stages— I'll say that much—we have here a cornucopia of disparities in which the questions and answers of sound nutrition still play at blind man's bluff. In harmonizing what felt like contradictions within myself, I have squeezed the rules out of the sense, and only the garden remains.

This book is set in Goudy Old Style, designed by F.W. Goudy in 1915. The face is modelled after Renaissance lettering.

Composed by WESType Publishing Services,
Boulder, Colorado.

Design by Barry Zaid.
Layout by Liza Matthews.

Printed and bound by Fairfield Graphics,
Fairfield, Pennsylvania.